WJEC A2 Law

Criminal Law and Justice

Study and Revision Guide

Louisa Walters
Karen Phillips
Sara Davies

Published in 2011 by Illuminate Publishing Ltd, P.O. Box 1160,
Cheltenham, Gloucestershire GL50 9RW

Orders: Please visit www.illuminatepublishing.com
or email sales@illuminatepublishing.com

British Library Cataloguing in Publication Data

A catalogue record for this book is available from the British Library

ISBN 978 0 9568401 3 4

Printed by 4edge Ltd., Hockley, Essex

03.14

This material has been endorsed by WJEC and offers high quality support for the
delivery of WJEC qualifications. While this material has been through a WJEC quality
assurance process, all responsibility for the content remains with the publisher.

Editor: Geoff Tuttle

Design Nigel Harriss

Layout: Claire Young

Permissions

p32, © fulloflove - Fotolia.com; p33, © vetkit - Fotolia.com; p35, © Serg Zastavkin -
Fotolia.com; p61, © RTimages - Fotolia.com; p63, ©HMG

Acknowledgements

The authors and publisher would like to thank:

Dr Pauline O'Hara for her thorough review of the book and expert insights and
observations.

Contents

How to use this book

This Study and Revision Guide is designed to guide you through the WJEC A Level Law specification and lead you to success in the subject. It has been written by senior examiners who have pinpointed exactly what is required of candidates in terms of content to achieve the highest marks. In addition, common errors have been identified and support and advice given in order that these can be avoided, which should lead to success in your A Level examination.

The Guide covers both A2 examination papers:

LA3 – Understanding Substantive Law: Criminal Law and Justice

LA4 – Understanding Law in Context: Criminal Law and Justice

The book is split into two sections.

Knowledge and Understanding

The **first section** of the book covers the knowledge content that is required for each topic within the A2 specification. This is written in a concise way and extension work is signposted, in order that you can get the best out of your revision.

Important features

Throughout the book, important cases are highlighted and underlined and important legal terms are emboldened for ease of reference at a glance.

Easy to use diagrams are used throughout to summarise information and make revision easier.

Synoptic Link

Suggested links to AS work are provided throughout the book, which are needed for revision as both LA3 and LA4 test synoptic knowledge from the AS specification. Possible suggestions are given in this feature.

Key terminology

Definitions of Key Terms are provided in an at-a-glance margin feature. All of these terms are key to the specification and should be learned.

Stretch and challenge

This feature gives you the opportunity to research the topic further and gives you advice on wider reading. These are usually current affairs or areas under reform; knowledge of which will really impress the examiner.

Grade boost

This feature gives you an insight into the examiners' minds and provides advice on things you should include to achieve the higher marks.

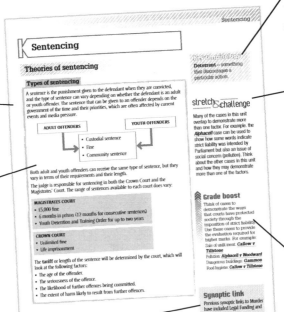

Exam Practice and Technique

This is the **second section** of the book and provides you with an opportunity for your own examination practice and an insight into the quality of answer that is expected to achieve a high grade. This section shows you an example of a Grade 'A' answer to a question as well as a Grade 'C/D' answer.

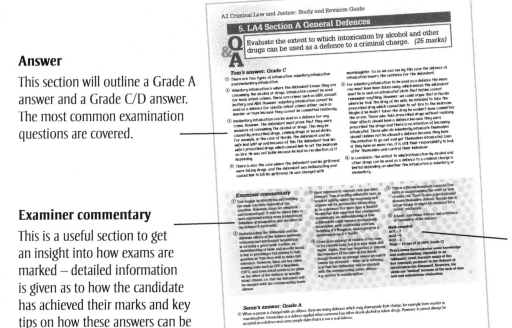

Answer

This section will outline a Grade A answer and a Grade C/D answer. The most common examination questions are covered.

Examiner commentary

This is a useful section to get an insight into how exams are marked – detailed information is given as to how the candidate has achieved their marks and key tips on how these answers can be improved.

Marks

The marks that would have been given to this candidate are split into the Assessment Objectives, so you can see how the exam answer has been marked.

Revision checklist

The table below gives an outline of the topics you can expect to see on each paper. You will notice that there are some topics which could appear on either paper. This means that you need to be able to apply the topic to either a problem scenario or an essay-stimulus response question.

	LA3	LA4
Defences	✓	✓
Homicide	✓	
Non-Fatal Offences	✓	✓
Police Powers	✓	
Strict Liability		✓
Criminal Procedure and Appeals	✓ (synoptic)	✓
Bail	✓ (synoptic)	✓
Crown Prosecution Service	✓ (synoptic)	✓
Sentencing – adults		✓
Sentencing – youths		✓

Knowledge and Understanding

LA3 & LA4: Criminal Law and Justice

LA3 focuses on developing students' understanding of substantive criminal law. The unit explores the elements of crime – *actus reus* and *mens rea* and then applies these concepts to the offences of murder, manslaughter and the non-fatal offences such as assault, battery, ABH, GBH and GBH with intent. It also explores how defences can negate criminal liability. The elements of the defences of intoxication, consent, insanity, self defence, necessity and mistake will be explored along with applying them to case scenarios to reach a conclusion. Special defences such as loss of control and diminished responsibility will be discussed in relation to murder and voluntary manslaughter. Students will then look at police powers in the areas of stop, search, arrest, detention, interrogation and admissibility of evidence before progressing on to consider the procedure for making a complaint against the police and the role of the IPCC. LA3 develops skills of applying the law to the facts of a case scenario in order to reach a conclusion, supported by legal authority. LA3 is synoptic and so the important links with certain topics studied at AS level are emphasised.

LA4 focuses on developing students' understanding of the elements of crime – *actus reus* and *mens rea*. It also looks at the elements of the general defences of intoxication by alcohol and other drugs, loss of control, diminished responsibility, mistake, self defence, duress, necessity, automatism, consent and insanity. It also requires students to understand strict liability and its advantages and criticisms. Students will then progress to look at the criminal procedure, appeals and the role of the CPS, DPP and Attorney General. Students explore magistrates' and judges' roles in sentencing and general principles of sentencing both adult and young offenders. LA4 looks to develop skills of essay writing and also stimulus response questions. LA4 is also synoptic and so the important links with AS topics are emphasised.

Revision checklist

Tick column 1 when you have completed brief revision notes.
Tick column 2 when you think you have a good grasp of the topic.
Tick column 3 during final revision when you feel you have mastery of the topic.

			1	2	3
Elements of Crime	p8	*Actus reus*			
	p10	*Mens rea*			
Homicide	p14	Murder			
	p17	Voluntary manslaughter			
	p21	Involuntary manslaughter			
Non-Fatal Offences Against the Person	p24	Hierarchy of offences			
	p25	Assault			
	p26	Battery			
	p26	S.47 - Actual bodily harm			
	p28	S.20 - Grievous bodily harm			
	p29	S.18 - Grievous bodily harm with intent			

K Elements of Crime

There are generally two elements required for the commission of a criminal offence – *actus reus* (the guilty act) and *mens rea* (the guilty mind). The general **presumption** is that a defendant must have committed a guilty act whilst having a guilty state of mind. This supports the Latin tenet: *actus non facit reum nisi mens sit rea*, which means the act does not make a person guilty unless the mind is also guilty. There are exceptions to this which will be explored in the chapter on Strict Liability. Once this is established, *causation* then needs to be proved which looks at the link between the result and the conduct of the defendant.

This unit will consider:
- *Actus reus* and omissions
- *Mens rea*
- Factual causation
- Legal causation.

Key terminology

Causation = often referred to as a '**chain of causation**' it connects the *actus reus* and the corresponding result. For there to be criminal liability, there must be an unbroken chain of causation.

Presumption = a presumption is a starting point for the courts. They presume certain facts to be true unless there is a greater preponderance of evidence to the contrary that rebuts the presumption.

≫ Pointer

Another case that demonstrates a 'state of affairs' crime is **Winzar v CC Kent (1983)**. In this case, the defendant was found drunk in a hospital and slumped on a chair. The police were called and removed him to the street where they charged him with being 'drunk on the highway' contrary to the Licensing Act 1872.

Actus reus

Latin for 'guilty act', it consists of all the elements of a crime other than the *mens rea*. *Actus reus* may consist of:

- **Conduct** – this action requires a particular conduct but the consequence of that behaviour is insignificant, e.g. perjury where a person lies under oath. It is irrelevant if the lie is believed or affects the case, the conduct of lying is sufficient as the *actus reus*.
- **Result** – this action requires a particular end result, e.g. murder. The crime requires the result of the victim dying. It also requires causation to be proved.
- **State of affairs** – for these crimes, the *actus reus* consists of 'being' rather than 'doing', e.g. 'being' in charge of a vehicle whilst under the influence of alcohol or drugs. There is a link with strict liability (explored later). This is demonstrated in the case of **R v Larsonneur (1933)**. Mrs Larsonneur, a French national, was brought to the UK from Ireland in police custody. This was done against her will and she had no desire to come to the UK. She was arrested on arrival in the UK for being an alien illegally in the UK. The fact she had not wanted to come to the UK, nor had any power over her transfer was irrelevant as she was 'found' or 'being' illegally in the UK. She was found guilty. These crimes are also known as **absolute liability** offences and are considered in the chapter on '**Strict Liability**'.
- **Omission** – a 'failure to act'. The general rule is that it is not an offence to fail to act unless under a **duty to act.** A person could walk past a random person drowning in a fountain and be under no legal obligation to help them out. The question of when a person has a duty to act will be considered below.

Duty to Act

A person can only be criminally liable if they have failed to act when under a legal duty to do so and the crime is capable of being committed by omission. There are recognised situations where a person *is* under a duty to act:

Statute – If a statute requires an action, it is unlawful not to do so. For example, under s.6 of the **_Road Traffic Act 1988_**, failing to provide a breath sample or a specimen for analysis is an offence.

Contract – Individuals may be contracted to act in a particular way and if they fail to act when under this contractual duty to do so, they may be liable for an offence. The case of **_R v Pitwood_** illustrates this.

Duty arising out of a special relationship – Certain family relationships result in a duty to act. For example, parent-child and spouses. The case of **_R v Gibbins and Proctor (1918)_** demonstrates this point.

Duty arising out of a person assuming responsibility for another – If a person chooses to take care of another person who is infirm or incapable of taking care of themselves, they are under a duty to do so without negligence. The case of **_R v Stone and Dobinson (1977)_** illustrates this. A more recent case is that of **_Evans (2009)_** where a mother and daughter were found guilty of manslaughter by their failure to call for help for the other daughter who had overdosed on heroin.

Defendant has inadvertently created a dangerous situation, becomes aware of it, but fails to take steps to rectify it – In the case of **_Miller (1983)_** the defendant was squatting in a flat. He fell asleep but had failed to extinguish his cigarette. When he awoke, he realised the mattress was alight but merely moved to the next room and went back to sleep. His failure to act and call for help caused hundreds of pounds of damage. He was convicted of arson.

The difference between a positive act and an omission

As stated above, it is generally not a crime to fail to act, unless under a duty to do so. For example, doing nothing while somebody drowns is an omission as opposed to holding that person's head under the water so that they drown, which is a positive act. In the case of **_Airedale NHS v Bland (1993)_** the removal of a feeding tube from a patient to allow him to die naturally was held to be an omission and therefore not a criminal act. Contrast this with euthanasia where an act such as administering a deliberate overdose in order to terminate a person's life would be classed as a positive act and therefore a criminal offence.

Another case where the defendant knew there was a dangerous situation but did not act is **_Santa-Bermudez (2003)_**.

1. _R v Pitwood (1902)_ In this case a carter was killed after Pitwood, a level crossing keeper, failed to close the crossing gate when he went to lunch. He had a contractual duty to ensure the crossing gate was closed and his failure to act led to the death of the carter.

2. _Gibbins and Proctor (1918)_. Defendant and his lover failed to feed his daughter who was living with them. She died as a result of starvation. The woman, despite the child not being hers, was living in the same household and had taken the defendant's money to feed the child. She was therefore under a duty to act (to feed and care for the child). They were both found guilty of murder.

3. _R v Stone and Dobinson (1977)_. Stone's younger sister, Fanny, came to live with Stone and Dobinson. Fanny suffered from anorexia and, despite some weak attempts by Stone and Dobinson to get her help, she eventually died. The jury found that a duty was assumed from electing to take care of a vulnerable adult. They should have made more of an effort to get her help and were found guilty of manslaughter.

Mens rea

As stated above, the general presumption is that a defendant must have committed a guilty act whilst having a guilty state of mind. **Mens rea** refers to the mental element in the definition of a crime. If Parliament intended *mens rea* in an offence it will often include *mens rea* words in the statute such as 'intentionally', 'recklessly' and 'negligently'. If Parliament deliberately left out a '*mens rea* word' then the offence may be considered to be one of **strict liability**.

The *mens rea* differs according to the crime. For example, the *mens rea* of **murder** is **malice aforethought**, which has come to mean an **intention to kill or cause GBH**, whereas the *mens rea* of assault is **intentionally** or **recklessly causing the victim to fear the application of immediate unlawful force**.

Coincidence of *actus reus* and *mens rea*

The general rule is that, to be guilty of a criminal offence requiring *mens rea*, an accused must possess the required *mens rea* when performing the *actus reus*, and it must relate to that particular act or omission. This is also known as the **Contemporaneity Rule**. For example, Bob is planning to kill his colleague tomorrow, but kills him by accident today. This does not make Bob guilty of murder.

There are two ways the courts have taken a flexible approach to this question:

1. **Continuing acts** – It is not necessary for *mens rea* to be present at the start of the *actus reus* as long as at some point in a continuous act, *mens rea* appears. The case of **Fagan v Metropolitan Police Commissioner (1969)** demonstrates this point. Fagan accidentally parked his car on a police officer's foot when asked by the officer to park the car near the curb. Fagan did not mean to drive his car on the officer's foot. However, when asked to move, he refused. It was at this point that *mens rea* was formed and driving onto the officer's foot and remaining there was a continuing act.

2. **Single transaction of events** – The courts have held that as long as there is one unbroken transaction of events then *actus reus* and *mens rea* need not occur at the same time. For example, if Rhidian attempts to murder Trystan by beating him to death but has not succeeded, then he *actually* kills Trystan by throwing what he assumes to be his corpse over a cliff, Rhidian will still be guilty of murder. In the case of **Thabo Meli (1954)** a similar situation arose. The defendants had attempted to kill the victim by beating him up but he was not dead. They then disposed of what they thought was his corpse over a cliff. The victim died as a result of the fall. The court held that there was one transaction of events and as long as the defendants had the relevant *mens rea* at the beginning of the transaction, it could coincide with the *actus reus* when that occurred.

Types of *Mens rea*

There are various types of *mens rea* but for the purposes of the WJEC specification, **Intention**, **Recklessness** and **Negligence** will be considered. It is important to appreciate that the specific *mens rea* required will depend on the offence being considered. For example, the *mens rea* of murder is **malice aforethought**, meaning an intention to kill or cause GBH, whereas the *mens rea* of battery is intention or recklessness to apply unlawful force. The *mens rea* is either defined in the relevant statute, as it is with s.47 assault occasioning actual bodily harm, or through case law, as is the case with oblique intent.

Intention

Intention is always **subjective**, meaning that in order to find that a defendant had intention, the court must believe that the particular defendant on trial desired the specific consequence of his action. To understand intention, it will be considered in relation to the offence of murder. The *mens rea* of murder is **malice aforethought.** Despite the term 'malice', no malice needs to be present. For example, murder could be committed out of love or compassion as in the case of helping a terminally ill relative in pain to die. In addition, no 'aforethought' is required either. Murder can be committed on the spur of the moment with no prior planning. According to **Vickers (1957),** the *mens rea* of murder can be implied from an intention to cause grievous bodily harm. A defendant does not need to have intended to kill. The definition has therefore been interpreted as **an intention to kill or cause GBH**. This will be explored further in the chapter on Murder.

There are two types of intention: **direct** and **oblique**.

Direct Intention is where the defendant has a clear foresight of the consequences of his action and specifically desires that consequence. For example, David stabs James because he desires the consequence of James' death.

Oblique Intention is less clear than direct intent. Here, the defendant may not actually desire the consequence of the action (e.g. death), but if he realises that the consequence will happen as a **virtual certainty**, he can be said to have oblique (or indirect) intention. This area of law has evolved through case law. The current direction on oblique intent comes from the case of **Nedrick (1986)** as confirmed in **Woolin (1998)**: ' *...the jury should be directed that they were not entitled to find the necessary intention for a conviction of murder unless they felt sure that death or serious bodily harm had been a virtual certainty (barring some unforeseen intervention) as a result of the defendant's actions and that the defendant had appreciated that such was the case, the decision being one for them to be reached on a consideration of all the evidence.'*

The judgement in **Woolin (1998)** has been further clarified in the more recent case of **Matthews and Alleyne (2003)**. The judge held that the test in **Woolin** is a rule of evidence and so the jury can decide, based on the facts, if they believe the defendant foresaw the consequence of death or serious injury as a virtually certainty but they do not have to.

Key terminology

Objective = based on what a **reasonable person** would do/think in the same position. In law, an objective test considers not the particular defendant in question, but what another average, reasonable person would have done/thought if placed in the same position as the defendant. There are occasions where some subjective characteristics of the defendant can be considered with an objective test (such as age and gender) that may have an effect on the way (s)he reacted.

Subjective = belonging to the individual in question (the subject). Intention is always subjective, meaning that to find intention, it must be believed that the particular defendant in question had the required intention in order to find him guilty of the offence.

stretch&challenge

The area of oblique intent has developed through case law over the years to the current direction provided on this page. Explore the following cases and consider their facts, how the law has changed and why. The following cases are in order of how the law has evolved:

- **Section 8 Criminal Justice Act 1967** – 'natural and probable consequence'.
- **R v Maloney (1985)** – 'natural consequence of the action'.
- **Hancock and Shankland (1986)** – 'degrees of probability'.
- **Nedrick (1986)**.
- **Woolin (1998)**.

Novus actus interveniens = this is an intervening act that is so independent of the original act of the defendant that it succeeds in breaking the chain of causation.

stretch&challenge

Explore the cases of *Cunningham (1957)* and *Caldwell (1982)*. What were the facts of the case and what did they rule in relation to negligence?

stretch&challenge

The standard of proof in a civil case is 'on the balance of probabilities' and the burden of proof is on the claimant.

Key case

R V G and another (2003). In this case, two boys aged 11 and 12 set fire to newspapers in a wheelie bin which was situated outside a shop. The fire spread to the shop and other buildings and caused one million pounds worth of damage. They were convicted of arson by the jury as, at the time, arson required an objective standard of recklessness (*Caldwell recklessness*) and the risk would have been obvious to a reasonable person, even if it was not to the young boys. On appeal, it was decided that the objective standard was not appropriate and the subjective characteristics of the boys such as their age and immaturity should be considered by the courts. As a result, Caldwell objective recklessness was overruled, replaced with subjective recklessness.

Recklessness

This type of *mens rea* concerns the taking of an unjustified risk. Following the case of *R v G and another (2003)* it is now almost purely a subjective concept, meaning that the prosecution must prove that the defendant realised (s)he was taking a risk.

The first use of the phrase 'subjective recklessness' was in the *Cunningham (1957)* case and is sometimes referred to as *Cunningham recklessness* where the court asks the question: '*was the risk in the defendant's mind at the time the crime was committed?*'.

Negligence

Negligence consists of falling below the standard of the ordinary reasonable person. The test is objective and has traditionally been associated with civil law. It now has some relevance in criminal law with *gross negligence manslaughter* as required by the WJEC specification. This will be explored later in this book.

The burden and standard of proof

In a criminal case, the burden of proving guilt is on the prosecution. The standard to which they need to prove this guilt is '*beyond reasonable doubt*'. The standard of proof is higher in a criminal case than a civil one as the impact of being found guilty of a criminal offence is much greater. It also supports the principle of '*innocent until proven guilty*'.

Causation

Causation relates to the causal relationship between conduct and result and is an important aspect of the *actus reus* of an offence. There needs to be an unbroken and direct *chain of causation* between the defendant's act and the consequences of that act. There mustn't be a *novus actus interveniens* that breaks the chain of causation else there will be no criminal liability for the resulting consequence.

There may be liability for the initial act. As with *mens rea*, above, this concept will be explored in relation to homicide.

There are two types of causation: *factual* and *legal*.

Factual causation	Legal causation

1. The '*but for*' test

This test asks 'but for' the conduct of the defendant, would the victim have died as and when he did? If the answer is no then the defendant will be liable for the death.

CASE: *R v White (1910)*. In this case, White poisoned his mother but she died of a heart attack before the poison had a chance to take effect. He was not liable for her death.

1. The injury must be the **operating and substantial cause of death**.

This test considers whether the original injury inflicted by the defendant is, at the time of death, still the operating and substantial cause of death.

CASE: *R v Smith (1959)*. Here, a soldier had been stabbed, dropped twice on his way to the hospital, delayed in seeing a doctor and subsequently given poor medical treatment. The court held that these other factors were not enough to break the chain of causation. At the time of death, the original wound was still the 'operating and substantial' cause of death.

CASE: *R v Jordan (1956)*. This case took a different stance to the *Smith* case above. In this case, the defendant stabbed the victim. Whilst in hospital, the victim was given an antibiotic to which he was allergic and died. The defendant was acquitted of murder because at the time of death, the original stab wound had almost healed and the death was attributable not to that, but to the antibiotic. The courts said that negligent medical treatment could only break the chain of causation where it is '**palpably wrong**'.

2. The *de minimis* rule

Meaning insignificant, minute, trifling; this test requires that the original injury caused by the defendant's action must be more than a minimal cause of death. See the Pagett Key case.

2. The '*thin skull*' test

A defendant has to take his victim as he finds him, meaning that if the victim dies due to some unusual or unexpected physical or other condition, the defendant is still responsible for the death. For example, if during a fight the defendant hits the victim with a punch that would not normally cause anything more than soreness and bruising, but, due to the victim having an unusually thin skull he dies, the defendant is still liable for the death.

CASE: *R v Blaue (1975)*. In this case, the defendant stabbed a woman who happened to be a Jehovah's witness. As a result of her beliefs she refused a blood transfusion which would have saved her life. The defendant argued he should not be responsible for her death as the transfusion could have saved her life and she refused it. The court disagreed and said he must take his victim as he finds her.

3. *Novus actus interveniens* – New intervening act

For an intervening act to break the chain of causation, it must be unforeseeable and random. It is sometimes likened to an 'act of God'. The case of *Jordan* above is an example of a *novus actus interveniens*.

Key terminology

Palpably wrong = In this context, 'palpably wrong' means really seriously wrong and so independent of the original act that it is possible to break the chain of causation. It was seen as a *novus actus interveniens* and the original stab wound was no longer the 'operating and substantial' cause of death.

Key case

Another case that demonstrates the 'but for test' and the '*de minimis rule*' is the case of *Pagett (1983)*. In this case, an armed defendant was trying to resist arrest and held his girlfriend in front of him as a human shield. He shot at the police and they shot back killing the girl. It was held that 'but for' his action of holding her as a human shield, she would not have died as and when she did. In addition, his action contributed significantly to her death. This was despite the fact it was not he who shot her.

stretch&challenge

A more recent case that looks at this issue is *Cheshire (1991)*. Find out about this case and what the court said in relation to causation.

⊼ Grade boost

The concepts explored in this chapter will be needed for each of the offences studied at A2 level. You will need to revisit this chapter when studying homicide and non-fatal offences and consider how it relates.

Homicide

stretch&challenge

Look up the case of *R v Cheshire (1991)*. This case also involved the question of whether substandard medical treatment was enough to break the chain of causation. Did the court agree with *R v Smith* or *R v Jordan*?

Synoptic link

Previous synoptic links to Murder have included Legal Funding and Appeal Routes.

Murder

This is the most serious of all the offences of homicide. The definition of murder is not contained in statute; indeed it is a common law offence, the definition of which was outlined by **Lord Justice Coke** in the seventeenth century:

'*The unlawful killing of a reasonable person in being and under the King's (or Queen's) Peace and with malice aforethought, express or implied.*'

Therefore, the elements in understandable terms are as follows.

Actus reus

1. A human being is dead.
2. The defendant caused the death IN FACT.
3. The defendant caused the death IN LAW.

Mens rea

Intention to kill or cause grievous bodily harm.
Intention can be DIRECT or INDIRECT.

Actus reus

1. A human being is dead.

A person is a human being when it can exist independent of its mother. Therefore, a person who kills an unborn child may be criminally liable under the law, but not for homicide. There is much controversy over what constitutes 'dead', but it would seem that the courts favour the definition of 'brain-dead' and this was confirmed in the case of *R v Malcherek and Steel (1981)*.

2. The defendant caused the death IN FACT.
3. The defendant caused the death IN LAW.

Mens rea

> ### INTENTION TO KILL *OR*
> ### INTENTION TO CAUSE GRIEVOUS BODILY HARM
> #### *DPP v Smith (1961)*:
>
> - The word 'grievous' means 'serious'.
> - The test of intention is **subjective**, which means that it is what the defendant intended, not what the reasonable man intended.

Direct intention

The defendant actually wants the death of the victim to occur and does what is necessary to achieve it.

Indirect intention

This is where the defendant foresaw the consequences, though did not want the consequences to happen.

CASE: *R v Moloney (1985)*. In this case, the defendant and his stepfather were larking around with a shotgun. Moloney pulled the trigger of the gun as a dare, and killed his stepfather.

He clearly had not intended to kill his stepfather, but would have foreseen that some serious harm or death could occur from pulling the trigger, and this was enough to show evidence of intention.

In relation to intention, the courts have been reluctant to devise a definitive rule, but a series of cases have indicated that the more foreseeable the result, the more likely it is that the defendant would have intended the outcome.

1975 *Hyam v DPP* – where there is foresight there will always be intention.

1986 *R v Hancock and Shankland (1986)* – the greater the probability of a consequence, the more likely the consequence was foreseen, and therefore also intended.

1986 *R v Nedrick* – judge directed that a jury can **infer** intention where death or grievous bodily harm is a **virtual certainty** of the defendant's actions.

1986 *R v Woollin* – changed the wording, so that a jury are entitled to **find** intention where death or grievous bodily harm is a **virtual certainty** of the defendant's actions. It is a question of evidence, not law.

2003 *R v Matthews and Alleyne* – followed the direction in *Woollin* and it now seems to be the correct approach to take.

Key cases

R v Hancock and Shankland (1986) – the defendants were miners who were on strike and threw a concrete block from a bridge killing a passing taxi driver.

R v Nedrick (1986) – the defendant was convicted of murder after throwing paraffin through the letterbox of a woman against whom he had a grudge. The woman's 12-year-old son died in the attack. An appeal was allowed and Nedrick was instead convicted of manslaughter. The court held that the jury should consider how probable the consequence was and whether it was foreseen by the defendant. The jury may then **infer** intention if they are confident that the defendant realised the consequence was a **virtual certainty**. See also cases on page 14.

See also cases on page 14.

stretch & challenge

If the courts are happy to conclude that indirect intention is still intention, think about cases of assisted suicide. Here, the person foresees that their actions will bring about the death of the person, even though that is not the result they would want. Look at the cases of ***Diane Pretty*** and ***Debbie Purdy***. Do you agree with the courts' decisions in these cases?

Research the case of ***Re A (Conjoined Twins) (2000)***. In this case, a life-saving operation for one Siamese twin would mean the other twin dying. Do you think this constitutes murder?

Grade boost

When applying the law to a problem question, take each element of the offence and apply to the problem question. Work your way methodically through this list of 'ingredients' applying them to the scenario and remembering to use appropriate legal authority throughout.

When assessing whether there is intention, bear in mind the proposals contained in the Law Commission report, *A New Homicide Act for England and Wales*? You should assess whether your conclusion would be different based on the new definition of intention.

Knowledge of the reforms on murder is essential for a potential question in Section B on the LA4 paper.

Reforms and criticisms of the law on murder

The Law Commission published a consultation paper in 2005 entitled *A New Homicide Act for England and Wales?* to review the law on murder. Its proposals are currently being considered by the Home Office.

1. It is proposed that there would be three tiers of homicide:

First degree murder	Second degree murder	Manslaughter
Mandatory life sentence	Discretionary life sentence	
• Intention to kill. • Intention to cause serious injury. • Defendant is aware that his conduct involves a risk of causing death.	• Intention to cause serious harm. • Intention to cause some injury with an awareness of the risk of death. • Intention to kill with a partial defence of provocation, diminished responsibility or duress.	• *Mens rea* of gross negligence. • Criminal act, where the defendant only intended harm, not serious harm. • Defendant appreciated the risk involved and foresaw a serious risk of causing injury.

2. Replace the common law approach to **intention** with a statutory definition. This would change the law slightly from *R v Woollin* because the jury will be able to use intention as part of the substantive law, and not just part of the evidence.

The Law Commission proposed that a statutory definition would read:
A person acts intentionally with respect to a result when he or she acts either:
   a) In order to bring it about; *or*
   b) Knowing that it will be virtually certain to occur; *or*
   c) Knowing that it would be virtually certain to occur if he or she were to succeed in his or her purpose of causing some other result.

We can therefore conclude that under the proposals, virtual certainty is intention, whereas lesser foresight is recklessness.

3. There was also a proposal to abolish the mandatory life sentence in order to deal with cases where the defences were being too leniently applied in order to give the judge discretion when sentencing the defendant. The government are reluctant to abolish the mandatory life sentence and this reform is unlikely to be implemented.

Voluntary manslaughter

Voluntary manslaughter
=

All elements of murder
+

Special defence:
• Loss of control; *or*
• Diminished responsibility; *or*
• Suicide pact.

Key terminology

Special defence = this is the use of a defence which has the effect not of completely acquitting the defendant but allowing a reduction in the sentence given to the defendant.

Voluntary manslaughter is the state of affairs where a defendant has committed murder but is relying on a **special defence** contained in the ***Homicide Act 1957*** and the ***Coroners and Justice Act 2009***. If the special defence is proved, the charge of murder will be reduced to manslaughter, and the judge will have discretion in terms of sentencing the defendant. The **burden of proof** is on the **defence** to prove that the defence applies to them.

Loss of control

It is important that a comparison is drawn here between this new defence contained in the ***Coroners and Justice Act 2009*** and the old defence of provocation which was contained in the ***Homicide Act 1957***.

	Provocation *s.3 Homicide Act 1957*	**Loss of control** *ss.54-56 Coroners and Justice Act 2009*
Critique	It was thought that this defence was harsh to victims of continued domestic violence. Under the new defence, a fear of violence can justify killing, and can be used by victims of continued domestic violence. It has been proved that women react more slowly to attack than men, therefore this defence was easier for men to rely on, because of the requirement of 'sudden' loss of control.	Under the new defence, a fear of violence can justify killing, and can be used by victims of continued domestic violence. The omission of the word 'sudden' in the defence makes it easier for women to rely on the defence where they have reacted slightly slower than a man would have.

stretch&challenge

Consider the cases of **R v Doughty (1986)**, **R v Pearson (1992)** and **R v Brown (1972)** above, which were decided under the old defence of provocation. How do you think they would be decided under the new defence?

R v Doughty (1986) – under the new defence, persistent crying of a baby does not equate to circumstances of an extremely grave character for trigger (ii).

R v Pearson (1992) – acts of third parties would be irrelevant for trigger (i), but may be relevant for trigger (ii).

R v Brown (1972) – the new Act is not clear about the situation where a mistake has been made, but this will be resolved by the courts in due course.

The use of this defence has implications of discrimination against women – the so-called *battered women syndrome* was brought to light in the cases of **Thornton** and **Ahluwalia**, which both involved women who killed their husbands after enduring years of abuse. In both cases there seemed to be a 'cooling off period' – which means the element of 'sudden' loss of control was not satisfied. It was raised in these cases that loss of control suddenly is a male reaction, and takes no account of the fact that women react to provocation in different ways.

Continued on next page.

	Provocation *s.3 Homicide Act 1957*	Loss of control *ss.54-56 Coroners and Justice Act 2009*
Elements of the defence	**1. Sudden and temporary loss of control** • The loss of control equated with a loss of temper – **R v Cocker (1989)**. • Sudden and temporary suggests no allowance of a 'cooling off' period – **R v Duffy (1949)** and **R v Ibrams (1982)**. • The court was lenient in allowing a time lapse between the provocation and the killing in the case of **R v Thornton (1992)**, but stopped short of allowing acts of revenge in the case of **R v Baille (1995)**.	**1. Loss of control** The loss of control here need not be sudden, which means that women with a 'slow-burn' reaction will not be treated less fairly.
Elements of the defence	**2. By things done or things said** • The persistent crying of a baby was held to amount to provocation in the case of **R v Doughty (1986)**. • A father who had subjected the defendant's brother to years of abuse was killed by the defendant in the case of **R v Pearson (1992)**, which shows that the provocation need not be directed at the defendant. • The case of **R v Brown (1972)** showed that a mistake made by the defendant that he was being attacked by a gang member did not have to be 'reasonable'.	**2. By a qualifying trigger** **s.55 Coroners and Justice Act 2009** suggests that this can be from: **(i)** A fear of serious violence from the victim. This is a new concept which protects women who have been subjected to continuous domestic violence by their abusive partners, or a homeowner who protected his property by killing a burglar. The test is **subjective**, which means it is how the defendant fears, not how the reasonable man or someone else in their position would fear the serious violence. s.55(3) suggests, however, that the victim has to be the source of violence, and the defendant has to fear the violence is directed towards them or another identified person.

	Provocation *s.3 Homicide Act 1957*	Loss of control *ss.54-56 Coroners and Justice Act 2009*
Elements of the defence		**(ii)** Things said or done of an extremely grave character causing the defendant a justifiable sense of being seriously wronged. This is a narrow approach because, although the sense of being wronged is subjective, this has to be justified, which is an objective test and one which can only be determined by the jury.
	3. Would a reasonable person have been provoked in the same way? • The case of ***DPP v Camplin (1978)*** held that the only characteristics relevant to compare to the reasonable person are those of age and sex. • In the case of ***R v Smith (Morgan) (2000)***, the House of Lords held that the jury can take into account abnormal characteristics of the defendant, such as depression, where those characteristics affect the standard of their control. • The case of ***A-G for Jersey v Holley (2005)*** is a contrast to this case because the court refused to take into account the disease of alcoholism as an 'abnormal characteristic'. The guidance given in this case was that the reasonable person must exercise the power of self-control expected of an ordinary person of like sex and age.	**3. Would a reasonable person have acted in the same way?** The new defence seems to have followed the case of ***A-G for Jersey v Holley (2005)*** since the guidance in ***s.54(1)(c)*** suggests that the defence is only available if a person of the defendant's sex and age, with a normal degree of tolerance and self-restraint and in the same circumstances as the defendant, might have reacted in the same way as the defendant. It is thought that where abnormal characteristics are present, it is more likely that the defendant will rely on the defence of diminished responsibility.
Burden of proof	The judge left the interpretation of the defence to the jury.	The prosecution must disprove the defence of loss of control beyond reasonable doubt.

Diminished responsibility

stretch&challenge

Another special defence to murder is that of **suicide pact**. It is for the defence to prove on the balance of probabilities that this defence applies. Look at the case of **R v H (2003)** – do you think that the reversal of the burden of proof disadvantages the defendant who is already likely to be distressed, or is it necessary to prevent disguised suicide pacts, for example those who assist someone to die to benefit from their death?

Grade boost

You need to be prepared for an essay question on LA4 on this topic as well as a problem question on LA3. The contemporary nature of this topic makes it highly examinable and you need to show an awareness of the changes and how they will affect defendants relying on these defences.

	Diminished responsibility *s.2 Homicide Act 1957*	Diminished responsibility as amended by *s.52 Coroners and Justice Act 2009*
Critique	The old defence did not allow medically recognised mental disorders.	The new definition of the defence means that one of the essential elements of the defence is a recognised medical condition.
Elements of the defence	**1a. The defendant suffered from an abnormality of the mind** This could be depression, 'mercy killing', pre-menstrual syndrome, and in the case of **R v Hobson (1997)** was held to amount to 'battered woman's syndrome'. **1b. The abnormality:** • arose from a condition of arrested or retarded development; *or* • any inherent causes; *or* • was induced by disease or injury.	**1. The defendant is suffering from an abnormality of mental functioning which arose from a recognised medical condition** This is a narrow definition but is a much more modern approach which takes into account an understanding of mental health issues. It is thought that some abnormalities of the mind under previous law may not succeed under the new defence because they are not recognised medical conditions. **CASE: R v Martin (Anthony) (2001)** would probably have succeeded under this defence because the defendant was suffering from a paranoid personality disorder when he killed an intruder in his home.
	2. The abnormality was a substantial cause of the defendant's act of killing Here, the defendant's abnormality needs to have been a substantial cause of the killing, but not necessarily the only cause. **CASE: R v Dietschmann (2003)** illustrates this because the defendant was suffering from depression, but was also drunk when he killed his victim. Even though the abnormality was the depression, the court accepted diminished responsibility because, even though he may not have killed had he been sober, the depression was a substantial cause.	**2. The abnormality of mental functioning must be a significant contributory factor to the killing** This means that the abnormality must cause, or at least be a significant contributory factor to the killing. If the case of **R v Dietschmann (2003)** were to be decided under the new defence, it is unclear whether the case would have got past the first hurdle of depression being recognised as a medical condition. However, it does seem to be the case that it does not matter if drink or drugs are involved; the key question is whether the medical condition overrides that and is a significant contributor to the killing.

	Diminished responsibility *s.2 Homicide Act 1957*	Diminished responsibility as amended by *s.52 Coroners and Justice Act 2009*
	3. The abnormality substantially impaired the defendant's mental responsibility for their acts	**3. The abnormality of mental functioning must have substantially impaired the defendant's ability to:** **a)** understand the nature of their conduct; *or* **b)** form a rational judgment; *or* **c)** exercise self-control This is a much more specific element of the crime and it makes clear what aspects of the mental functioning must be affected.
Burden of proof		The defence must prove that the defendant was suffering from diminished responsibility at the time of the offence on the balance of probabilities. Expert evidence is required from at least two witnesses.

Key case

Key Case – Wood (2008)

In this case it was held that alcohol dependency syndrome and the effect of this on the defendant could be considered as an abnormality of the mind (now abnormality of mental functioning) by the jury.

Involuntary manslaughter

Involuntary manslaughter
=
Only *actus reus* of murder
+
1) Unlawful and dangerous act *OR* **2)** Gross negligence

Involuntary manslaughter is the state of affairs where a defendant has committed the *actus reus* of murder but not the *mens rea*.

	Unlawful and dangerous act manslaughter also known as constructive manslaughter
Actus reus	**All common elements of murder**

stretch&challenge

Consider the case of **R v Lamb (1967)**, where the defendant pointed a gun at his friend as a joke. The defendant had no intention of hurting the victim, but one of the bullets slipped out and killed his friend. Can you identify: a) the unlawful act and b) the *mens rea* of that act? Based on this, is the defendant guilty of constructive manslaughter?

Unlawful and dangerous act manslaughter also known as constructive manslaughter

Actus reus

An unlawful act

- Has to be an act; not an omission.

CASE: R v Lowe (1973) involved the commission of the offence of child neglect, and the neglect caused the child's death.

- The act has to be 'criminal'; not civil. This was held in the case of **R v Franklin (1883)**.

CASE: R v D (2006) The victim, having suffered years of domestic abuse from her husband, committed suicide. Prior to the suicide, her husband had cut her forehead when he struck her with his bracelet. This was held to be enough of an unlawful criminal act because it constituted an offence under **s.20 Offences Against the Person Act 1861**.

A dangerous act

- The test is whether a reasonable person would foresee that the act would cause harm.

CASE: R v Church (1966) held that the test has to be whether a 'sober and reasonable person would realise the risk' of their act.

- It must be the case that the defendant has the same knowledge as the sober and reasonable person.

CASE: R v Dawson (1985) the victim was a 60-year-old person with a serious heart condition. The defendants were not to know this and neither was a sober and reasonable person. Therefore the act cannot be dangerous.

CASE: R v Watson (1989) in this case, the victim was an 87-year-old man. The court held that the defendants should be reasonably expected to know that the man would be frail and easily scared, therefore the act was dangerous.

Causation

- It must be established that the unlawful and dangerous act was the cause of the death.

CASE: R v Johnstone (2007) – the victim was subjected to a series of taunts which involved:
  - spitting and shouting (not deemed to be a dangerous act)
  - stones and wood being thrown (deemed to be a dangerous act).

The victim then suffered a heart attack brought on by stress. The defendants could not be convicted of constructive manslaughter because it was not clear whether it was the dangerous act that brought on the heart attack, and thus caused the death of the victim.

- If the victim intervenes himself into the chain of causation with a voluntary act, then this will be sufficient to break the chain of causation.

CASE: R v Kennedy (No 2) (2007) – in this case the court held that a drug dealer can never be held responsible for the death of a drug user. Contrast this case:

CASE: R v Cato (1976) – this is a contrasting case because the dealer injected the heroin into the victim. In this case, the defendant would have been liable for the manslaughter of the victim.

Unlawful and dangerous act manslaughter also known as constructive manslaughter

Mens rea

The *mens rea* for this offence is the *mens rea* of the unlawful act.

For example, if the unlawful act was **s.47 Offences Against the Person Act 1861**, then the *mens rea* would be either recklessness or intention to either cause the victim to fear the immediate application of unlawful force or to apply unlawful force.

Gross negligence manslaughter

The test was laid down in the case of *R v Adomako (1994)*

All common elements of murder

Duty of care

- A duty of care is established under the 'neighbourhood principle' contained in **Donoghue v Stevenson (1932)**.
- Whether or not a duty of care is owed is a matter for the jury to decide using the 'neighbourhood principle'.
- A few key exceptions arose in **R v Willoughby (2004)** where it was held that there will almost always be a duty of care between doctor and patient.

Gross negligent breach of that duty

- Whether or not the breach of the duty amounts to gross negligence is a matter for the jury to decide, though in the case of **R v Bateman (1925)**, Lord Hewart CJ suggested that it '*showed such disregard for life and safety of others as to amount to a crime against the State and conduct deserving punishment*'.

Risk of death

As well as being expressed in **R v Adomako (1994)**, this provision was further confirmed in **R v Misra and Srivastava (2005)** where doctors failed to diagnose a post-operation infection which led to the death of the patient. The lack of diagnosis and the subsequent lack of treatment were held to constitute a risk of death.

Non-Fatal Offences Against the Person

Hierarchy of offences

The majority of offences do not result in death. There are five non-fatal offences against the person that need to be considered for WJEC A2 Criminal Law and Justice. They form a large part of the A2 exam and are frequently combined with **general defences**.

They can be examined in both papers LA3 and LA4. It is important to be aware of the *actus reus* and *mens rea* of each offence with case law to support.

It is important to appreciate the hierarchical relationship between the offences, as **plea bargaining** can happen between offences. Plea bargaining is an agreement in a criminal case between prosecution and defence that the charge will be reduced if the defendant pleads guilty. For example, a defendant charged with a s.20 offence will be offered the opportunity to plead guilty to the lesser s.47 offence. On the face of it, this seems unfair and not in the interests of justice but the courts rely upon defendants pleading guilty.

From least serious to most:

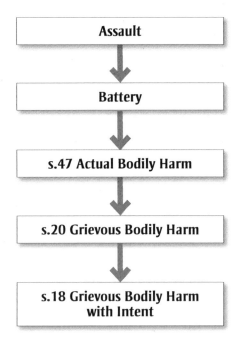

The CPS **Charging Standards** provides guidance to prosecutors as to what injuries constitute which non-fatal offence. It doesn't, however, have any legal significance and is merely there to guide.

Each of the offences will now be considered in turn.

Assault

Assault is not defined in an Act of Parliament, as it is a **common law** offence. s.39 of the **Criminal Justice Act 1988** provides that assault is a **summary offence** with a maximum sentence on conviction of six months' imprisonment or a fine.

Actus reus

The *actus reus* of assault is any act which causes the victim to apprehend the immediate infliction of unlawful violence, e.g. raising a fist, pointing a gun or threatening somebody. In the case of **Logdon v DPP (1976)**, as a joke, the defendant pointed a gun at the victim. She was frightened until he told her it was a replica gun. The court held that the victim had apprehended immediate physical violence, and the defendant had been at least reckless as to whether this would occur.

Words can amount to an assault, as can silent telephone calls. In the case of **R v Ireland, Burstow (1997)** the defendant made silent telephone calls to three women and these were held to be sufficient to cause the victim to apprehend the immediate infliction of unlawful force. In **Constanza (1997)** threatening letters were held to amount to an assault. Words can also take away liability for assault as in the case of **Tuberville v Savage (1669)** where the accused put his hand on his sword and said 'If it were not **assize** time I would not take such language from you.' The threat was the hand being placed on the sword which could have amounted to an assault; however, because he coupled this with the statement that he would not use his sword as it was assize time, this meant that the words took away liability for the assault.

The threat has to be 'immediate' though this has been interpreted liberally by the courts, as can be evidenced by the cases of **Ireland** and **Constanza** above. In the case of **Smith v Chief Superintendent of Woking Police Station (1983)** the victim was in her nightdress in her downstairs window. The defendant who had trespassed on to her property was staring at her through the window and even though the door was locked and she was behind the window, it was sufficiently 'immediate' for an assault.

Mens rea

The *mens rea* of assault as defined in the case of **R v Savage, Parmenter (1992)** is that the defendant must have either intended to cause the victim to fear the infliction of immediate and unlawful force, or must have foreseen the risk that such fear would be created (**subjective recklessness**).

Key terminology

Occasioning = to bring about; cause.

Omission = a failure to act which can impose criminal liability when under a duty to act.

Triable either way = mid-range offences that can be tried either in the Magistrates' Court or the Crown Court depending on the gravity of the offence and the plea of the defendant.

stretch&challenge

Though assault and battery are two separate and distinct offences, they can sometimes be charged together as 'common assault'.

stretch&challenge

Research the case of **Wood (Fraser) v DPP (2008)**. Apply the *actus reus* and *mens rea* of battery to the facts.

Battery

As with assault, battery is not defined in an Act of Parliament; it is a **common law** offence. s.39 of the **Criminal Justice Act 1988** provides that battery is a **summary offence** with a maximum sentence on conviction of six months' imprisonment or a fine.

Actus reus

The *actus reus* of battery is the application of unlawful physical force on another. It is accepted that a certain amount of physical force happens in daily life (**Collins v Wilcock (1984)**, such as walking down a busy street where people may bump in to one another. For it to be a battery, the force must be unlawful. The application does not need to be direct as in the case of **Haysted v DPP (2000)** where the defendant punched a woman causing her to drop her child. It was held to be indirect battery of the child. Similarly, in the case of **Fagan v Metropolitan Police Commissioner (1969)** Fagan accidentally parked his car on a police officer's foot when asked by the officer to park the car near the curb. Fagan did not mean to drive his car on the officer's foot. However, when asked to move, he refused. The force was applied indirectly by the car driving on to the officer's foot and was unlawful when he refused to move.

The term 'physical force' implies that a high level of force needs to be applied, but this isn't the case. In the case of **Thomas (1985)** it was held that touching the hem of a girl's skirt whilst she was wearing it was akin to touching the girl herself. The victim also need not be aware that he or she is about to be struck; therefore, if someone is struck from behind this will still constitute battery. Contrast this with assault where the victim must fear the application of unlawful force and so therefore must be aware of it.

Unlike assault, a battery can be committed by **omission** where there is a duty to act.

In the case of **DPP v Santana-Bermudez (2004)** the defendant was asked by a police officer searching him whether he had any 'needles or sharps' on him. He failed to inform her and when she searched him she pricked her finger on a hypodermic needle in his pocket. It was held that his failure to inform her of the presence of the needle was sufficient to satisfy the *actus reus*.

Mens rea

The *mens rea* of battery is intention or subjective recklessness to apply unlawful force on another as confirmed in of **R v Venna (1976)**.

S.47 Actual bodily harm

The statutory offence of actual bodily harm is set out in **s.47 Offences Against the Person Act 1861** which provides that it is an offence to commit an assault **occasioning** actual bodily harm.

Although the statute only refers to assault, the offence may also be committed by a battery. It is in fact far more common for offences under s.47 to be committed by battery rather than by an assault. Actual bodily harm is a **triable either way** offence. The maximum sentence for ABH is five years' imprisonment.

Actus reus

The *actus reus* for ABH can be broken down into three elements:

1. Assault or battery

2. Occasioning

3. Actual bodily harm

1. **Assault or battery** – The first element of ABH requires proof of the *actus reus* of either an assault or battery as defined above.

2. **Occasioning** – the assault or battery must occasion, i.e. *cause*, actual bodily harm. The **chain of causation** therefore needs to be established between the defendant's act and the harm caused.

   This is usually easy to prove but in the case of ***R v Roberts (1971)*** a girl jumped from a moving car injuring herself, and the question was asked whether the fact that she had chosen to jump from the moving car broke the chain of causation. She did this as the defendant was making sexual advances towards her including touching her clothes. It was held that the defendant had committed a battery by touching the girl's clothes and that had caused her to jump out of the moving car thereby injuring herself. It was stated in the case that the victim's reaction (jumping from the car) did not break the chain of causation if it was reasonably foreseeable provided it was not *so 'daft or so unexpected that no reasonable man could be expected to foresee it'*. If this was the case then it could constitute a ***novus actus interveniens***.

3. **Actual bodily harm** – this can be physical or psychological harm as held in the case of ***Miller (1954)***. It can include cutting someone's hair as in ***DPP v Smith (2006)***. The definition of what constitutes ABH has been clarified in the case of ***Miller (1954)*** as 'hurt or injury calculated to interfere with health or comfort'. The case of ***Chan Fook (1994)*** also makes the point that the injury needs to be more than 'transient or trifling'. The word 'actual' in this context means that though the injury doesn't need to be permanent, it should not be so trivial as to be insignificant. The case of ***DPP v Smith (Michael) (2006)*** confirmed that cutting off a large amount of hair could be considered to be 'actual bodily harm'.

Mens rea

The *mens rea* is the same as for assault or battery. There is no requirement to prove any extra *mens rea* for the actual bodily harm as per the case of ***Roberts (1971)***. The case of ***R v Savage (1992)*** confirmed this.

Key case

R v Savage (1992) – In this important case, a woman went into a bar where she saw her ex's new girlfriend. She went up to her and said, 'nice to meet you darling' and threw beer from her glass over her. On doing so, she accidentally let go of the glass which broke, cutting the new girlfriend's wrist. She argued that she had only the *mens rea* of battery (throwing the beer) but the court held that this was irrelevant. No additional *mens rea* was required for the actual bodily harm (the glass cutting the woman's wrist). As long as she had the *mens rea* for battery then the *mens rea* of ABH was satisfied.

Key terminology

Chain of causation = connects the *actus reus* and the corresponding result. For there to be criminal liability, there must be an unbroken chain of causation.

Novus actus interveniens = a new intervening act. This is an intervening act that is so independent of the original act of the defendant that it succeeds in breaking the chain of causation.

Grade boost

Here you could state what the *mens rea* of assault or battery actually is:

Assault – Intention or subjective recklessness to cause the victim to apprehend the infliction of immediate unlawful violence.

Battery – Intention or subjective recklessness to apply unlawful force on the victim.

Grievous = defined in *DPP v Smith (1961)* as 'really serious harm'. Confirmed in *Saunders (1985)*. In the case of *R v Brown and Stratton (1998)* injuries such as bruising, broken nose, missing teeth and concussion were held to be grievous bodily harm.

Maliciously = is interpreted as meaning with intention or subjective recklessness.

Wounding = where both layers of the skin are broken usually resulting in bleeding.

stretch&challenge

The cases of *Clarence* and *Dica* are also discussed in the topic on general defences. Consider how the issue of consent may be relevant here.

Clarence (1888) – In this case it was ruled that 'inflict' required an assault or battery and as she had consented to the sexual intercourse, neither of these was present. This is now considered to be bad law.

stretch&challenge

The leading case is now: *R v Savage; DPP v Parmenter* that confirmed this point.

S.20 Grievous bodily harm

The statutory offence of grievous bodily harm is set out in *s.20 Offences Against the Person Act 1861*, which provides that it is an offence to **maliciously** inflict **grievous** bodily harm or **wound** the victim.

Grievous bodily harm is a **triable either way** offence. The maximum sentence for GBH is five years' imprisonment, the same as for the lesser offence of ABH, which has been criticised.

Actus reus

GBH can be proved by either showing an **infliction** of grievous bodily harm or a **wounding** of the victim.

It is important to choose the charge carefully as being *either* infliction of GBH *or* a wound.

1. **Infliction of GBH** – The term 'inflict' has caused difficulty in the courts over the years. In the case of *Clarence (1888)* the term was given a very restrictive meaning but more recently in *Dica (2004)* the meaning was widened to include recklessly transmitting HIV to an unaware victim as being 'infliction' of GBH. A similarly wide approach is demonstrated in *R v Halliday (1889)* where a husband frightened his wife to the extent that she jumped out of their bedroom window to escape. The court held that her injuries had been directly inflicted by the defendant even though it was she who had voluntarily jumped from the window. The case of *R v Bollom (2003)* established that the age and characteristics of the victim are relevant to the extent of the injuries sustained.

2. **Wounding** – A wound requires a breaking in the continuity of the skin usually resulting in bleeding. In the case of *Moriarty v Brooks (1834)* it was held that both the dermis and the epidermis must be broken; however, in the case of *JCC (A Minor) v Eisenhower (1984)* an internal rupture of blood vessels in the victim's eye as a result of being shot with a pellet gun was not held to amount to wounding within s.20.

A scratch or break to the outer skin is not sufficient if the inner skin remains intact *M'Loughlin (1838)*.

Mens rea

The *mens rea* for GBH is defined by the word **maliciously**.

The case of *Mowatt (1967)* established that it does not need to be established whether or not the defendant intended or was reckless as to the infliction of GBH or a wound as long as it can be proved that he intended or was reckless to cause *some physical harm*. This was further clarified in the case of *DPP v A (2000)* where it was held to be sufficient to prove the defendant intended or foresaw that some harm *might* occur and it was not necessary to show the defendant intended or foresaw that some harm *would* occur.

S.18 GBH with intent

The statutory offence of grievous bodily harm with intent is set out in **s.18 Offences Against the Person Act 1861** which provides that it is an offence to **intend** to maliciously wound or cause grievous bodily harm. S.18 is an **indictable** offence.

The maximum sentence for s.18 is life imprisonment, reflecting the gravity of s.18 in comparison to s.20.

Actus reus

Similar to the *actus reus* for s.20, the *actus reus* for s.18 is either maliciously wounding or causing grievous bodily harm. It refers to the term 'cause' as opposed to 'inflict' and though they are not the same (**R v Ireland, Burstow (1997)**) they have been taken to mean that causation is required. The meaning of 'wound' and causing 'grievous bodily harm' are the same as for s.20 above.

Mens rea

The key difference between s.20 and s.18 is that s.18 can only be proved with intention (direct or oblique) whereas s.20 can be established with recklessness or intention to cause *some* harm. The *mens rea* has two aspects: firstly, the defendant must 'maliciously' wound or cause grievous bodily harm. Secondly, the defendant must have specific intent to either cause grievous bodily harm to the victim or to resist or prevent the lawful apprehension or detention of any person.

s.18 is a **specific intent offence** (as required by **R v Belfon (1976)**) and requires intention to **maliciously** cause *grievous* bodily harm, thus reflecting the severity of the injuries and culpability of the defendant.

Charging Standards

The CPS has issued guidelines known as 'charging standards' for the offences against the person to ensure greater consistency. It details types of injury (e.g. swelling, graze, black eye, etc.) and the charge that should follow if such injuries are present.

Key terminology

Indictable = the most serious offences triable only in the Crown Court.

stretch&challenge

s.18 is a crime of **specific intent**, meaning that it can only be proved with intention as the *mens rea*. s.47 and s.20 are both **basic intent** offences as they can be proved with either intention or recklessness.

stretch&challenge

Have a look at the Charging Standards on the CPS website and make a list of the likely injuries for each of the offences mentioned in this chapter.

General Defences

Complete defence = the successful use of this defence results in the defendant being completely acquitted of the offence. Examples include self defence or insanity.

Partial defence = the successful use of this defence results in conviction for a lesser offence. For example, successful use of diminished responsibility reduces a charge of murder to manslaughter.

Grade boost

This is a very important topic as it can feature on both LA3 and LA4. Therefore, you must be able to apply the law to a problem scenario OR provide a detailed explanation and analysis as part of an essay-based question.

Where a defendant is to stand trial for an offence, he or she may rely on a defence to the crime, which will have the effect of lowering the offence, reducing the sentence, or in some cases, totally acquit the defendant of all charges.

As a general rule, in criminal cases, the burden of proof is on the prosecution to prove beyond reasonable doubt that the defendant committed the crime. However, where a defence is raised, this burden of proof is often reversed and the onus is on the defence to provide some evidential proof that the defendant can rely on the defence. Once the evidence is produced to prove the existence of the defence, the burden of proof then reverts back to the prosecution to disprove the evidence and convince the jury that the defence does not apply to the defendant.

Types of defences, burden of proof and result of defence can be summarised thus:

Defence	Burden of proof	Result for defendant where successful
Non-insane automatism	Defence has to produce evidence to support defence and the prosecution then has to disprove the evidence.	• Complete defence for specific intent crimes; and • Complete defence for basic intent crimes where the automatism is not self-induced.
Intoxication		Can be a complete defence; so long as required *mens rea* has not been formed.
Self defence		Complete defence
Duress		Complete defence
Insanity	Defence has to produce evidence to support the defence AND prove to the jury that the defence existed.	Complete defence • Under the ***Criminal Procedure (Insanity and Unfitness to Plead) Act 1991***, the court may make: **a)** Hospital Order **b)** Supervision Order **c)** Absolute Discharge
Consent	Prosecution has to prove that the defendant did not consent to the harm.	Complete defence

Insanity

It must be noted that everyone is presumed to be sane. Where a defendant pleads insanity, it means that they believe they were insane at the time the offence was committed, not when they stand trial. There are essentially three elements to the defence, and these elements were laid down in the case of *M'Naghten (1843)*:

1. Defect of reason	This means that you are devoid of the power to reason, rather than just failing to use this power. **CASE: *R v Clarke (1972)*** – here the defendant was accused of shoplifting, and argued that she was acting absentmindedly because of depression. The court held that absentmindedness or confusion did not equate to insanity.
2. Disease of the mind	The defect of reason has to be caused by a disease of the mind, and that disease has to be an INTERNAL cause. This is a legal term, and not a medical one, so the identification of a psychiatric illness is not enough. Examples of diseases of the mind have included: Contrast these two cases:
Diabetes	**CASE: *R v Quick (1973)*** – the defendant was a diabetic who had taken his insulin, but had not eaten enough afterwards. Court – this is NOT INSANITY because the cause of the insanity was the insulin which is an EXTERNAL factor. **CASE: *R v Hennessey (1989)*** – the defendant was a diabetic who had not taken his insulin which resulted in hyperglycaemia. Court – this is INSANITY because there were not external factors; the disease, diabetes, is an internal factor.
Sleepwalking	This is also an internal cause, and there have been many cases involving defendants who had been sleepwalking and successfully pleaded insanity. **CASE: *R v Burgess (1991)*** – the defendant and his girlfriend had been watching videos and in his sleep, Burgess killed the girl. Once again, there was no evidence of external factors, so he successfully pleaded insanity due to an internal cause; the sleep disorder.
Epilepsy	**CASE: *R v Sullivan (1984)*** – the defendant had suffered from epilepsy since being a child, and during a particularly aggressive fit, he attacked and injured an 80-year-old man. He successfully used the defence of insanity.
3a. Not know the nature and quality of his act *OR*	This may mean that the defendant was in a state of unconsciousness, or did not know the physical nature and quality. **CASE: *R v Codere (1916)*** – the defendant slit the victim's throat under the illusion that it was a loaf of bread.
3b. Lacked knowledge that the act was wrong	This definition again covers a legal wrong, rather than a moral wrong. **CASE: *R v Windle (1952)*** – the defendant in this case killed his wife, and afterwards declared 'I suppose they will hang me for this'. Although he was suffering from a mental illness, he still knew that his actions were legally wrong so his defence of insanity failed.

Key case

M'Naghten (1843) – in this case, the defendant had an obsession with the Prime Minister of the time, Sir Robert Peel. He tried to kill Peel, but instead killed his secretary. He stood trial for the murder of the secretary but was found not guilty by reason of insanity.

Grade boost

Remember that INsanity has to be caused by an INternal factor. This is important as insanity is very often confused with non-insane automatism which is caused by an external factor.

stretch&challenge

Research the case of *R v Thomas (2009)*, which involved a man from Neath in South Wales who killed his wife in his sleep because of a rare sleep disorder. Do you think it is wrong that these people are labelled with a stigma of 'disease of the mind' and 'insane', when in fact they can usually be controlled with medication? Think of some other criticisms of this defence.

stretch&challenge

Look up the more recent case of *Johnson (2007)* where the decision in *Windle* was followed.

Automatism

Non-insane automatism has to be caused by an EXTERNAL factor over which the defendant has no control.

Bratty v Attorney General for Northern Ireland (1963)

'An act done by the muscles without any control by the mind, such as a spasm, a reflex action or convulsion; or an act done by a person who is not conscious of what he is doing such as an act done whilst suffering from concussion or whilst sleep-walking.'

Some external factors that could be covered by this definition include sneezing, hypnotism, automatism and the unknown effects of a drug or a blow to the head. In the case of **Hill v Baxter (1958)**, a plea of automatism was successful where the defendant had been attacked by a swarm of bees whilst driving.

It has also been the case that exceptional stress can amount to automatism. This was illustrated in the case of **R v T (1990)**, where the defendant stabbed the victim whilst suffering from severe post traumatic stress disorder. Although the judge allowed the defence, the jury were not convinced and convicted the defendant.

However, this defence has been known to have rather harsh application at times:

CASE: Broome v Perkins (1987) – in this case, the defendant was in a hyperglycaemic state and drove home from work erratically which caused significant damage to his car. He could remember nothing about the journey, but the court held that because it was a familiar journey, someone in his state should have been able to get home safely, because there was evidence that some of his actions could have been voluntarily controlled. Therefore, the defence of automatism was not available.

In order for this offence to be successfully used, it must first of all be distinguished whether the crime in question is one of **specific intent** or **basic intent**. If the defence is proved, then it is a complete defence and the defendant will be free to go.

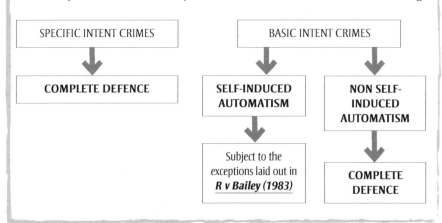

Key terminology

Basic intent = where the *mens rea* for a crime is recklessness or negligence, or a crime of strict liability. Examples include all offences under the **Offences Against the Person Act 1861**, with the exception of **s.18**, and for which automatism will be a complete defence provided it was not self-induced.

Specific intent = where the *mens rea* for a crime is one of intention. Examples include murder and **s.18 Offences Against the Person Act 1861** which is grievous bodily harm with intent, and for which automatism will be a complete defence.

stretch&challenge

Revisit the cases of **R v Quick (1973)** and **R v Hennessey (1989)**. Could Quick have used the defence of automatism? Give reasons for your answer.

Self-induced automatism

Where a person knowingly becomes an automaton, in other words he knows that his actions are likely to bring about an automatic state and he commits a **basic intent** offence, the rules are slightly different. The defence will always be available for **specific intent** crimes because it would be unfair to convict a defendant who does not have the required *mens rea* for an offence.

For self-induced automatism, where a basic intent crime is committed, the rules were laid down in **R v Bailey (1983)**. This case outlined that automatism cannot be a defence, where:

a) The defendant has been reckless in becoming an automaton; or

b) Where the automatism has been caused by illegal drink or drugs.

However, the judge in the case did stipulate that the defence of automatism CAN BE USED where:

c) The defendant does not know that his actions are likely to result in an automatic state. This is because it cannot be said that the defendant has been reckless in becoming an automaton.

CASE: R v Hardie (1994) – the defendant was depressed because of a relationship split, and took some Valium that had been prescribed for his former girlfriend. She encouraged him to take them to calm him down, but unknown to him they had the opposite effect and he set fire to a wardrobe. The judge allowed the defence of automatism because he had not been reckless in getting into that state.

Intoxication

This defence covers situations where the defendant has committed an offence whilst under the influence of alcohol or drugs. There are two questions that need to be asked to establish the existence of the defence:

Was the intoxication **voluntary** or **involuntary**?

Was the crime one of **basic intent** or **specific intent**?

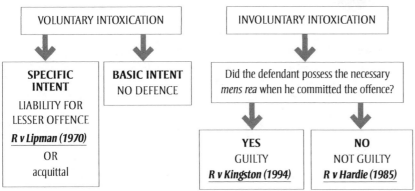

Key terminology

Involuntary intoxication = this is where the defendant unknowingly becomes intoxicated through, for example, a drink being spiked or the unknown side effects of a prescribed drug. In these circumstances, the court must ascertain whether the defendant possessed the required *mens rea* for the offence in question.

Voluntary intoxication = this is where the defendant willingly and knowingly becomes intoxicated. This is regarded as a reckless course of conduct and will affect the defendant's use of the defence if the offence that has been committed is one of basic intent.

Key case

R v Bailey (1983) – the defendant was a diabetic who had failed to eat enough after taking his insulin. He became aggressive and hit someone over the head with an iron bar. The court held that the defence of automatism was not available because the defendant was reckless in becoming an automaton.

Grade boost

It is always a good idea, when dealing with intoxication in a problem question to make a note of:

The type of offence that has been committed in the scenario (basic intent or specific intent).

Whether the intoxication was **voluntary** or **involuntary**.

Basic intent crimes
= crimes which require anything other than intention as *mens rea*, for example, involuntary manslaughter, all non-fatal offences against the person, except *s.18 Offences Against the Person Act 1861*.

Specific intent crimes
= crimes which require intention as their *mens rea*; for example, murder. Where voluntary intoxication is being used as a defence for these crimes, it is likely that the defendant will be charged with the corresponding lesser offence.

Key case

R v Lipman (1970) – the defendant and his girlfriend had taken LSD before falling asleep. As a result of drug-induced hallucinations, the defendant thought he was at the centre of the earth being attacked by snakes. When he awoke, he found his girlfriend dead because he had strangled her and stuffed a sheet in her mouth, believing her to be one of the snakes attacking him.

Voluntary intoxication and basic intent crimes

For crimes of basic intent, the defence of voluntary intoxication is not available, because the court takes the approach that becoming intoxicated is in itself a reckless course of conduct, and this is therefore enough to form the required *mens rea* of any basic intent offence.

CASE: _DPP v Majewski (1977)_ – the defendants had spent over 24 hours drinking alcohol and taking drugs, and then caused serious criminal damage and assaulted a police officer. It was argued that due to his intoxicated state, Majewski could not remember committing the criminal acts. The court held that, because his crimes were basic intent, he could not rely on the defence.

Voluntary intoxication and specific intent crimes

For most offences, there is a corresponding lesser offence, so where the defendant uses the defence of intoxication for a specific intent offence, they will not have a complete defence, but will be charged with the lesser, basic intent offence.

For example:

Murder		Manslaughter	
s.18 Offences Against the Person Act 1861	→	*s.20 Offences Against the Person Act 1861*	*R v Lipman (1970)* *R v Bratty (1963)*

Where there is no corresponding basic intent offence, the defendant will be able to rely on intoxication as a complete defence, as the court will take the approach that the defendant could not have formed the correct *mens rea* for the specific intent crime, and if there is no alternative, there is nothing with which the defendant can be convicted.

The leading case here is **_DPP v Beard (1920)_**, where the defendant was charged with murder and had raised the defence of intoxication to support the fact that he could not form the *mens rea* for the crime. In allowing the defence, Lord Birkenhead formulated the stance that has been taken for specific intent crimes since:

'*If he was so drunk that he was incapable of forming the intent required, he could **not** be convicted of a crime which was committed only if intent was proved.*'

However, what is critical is that even though intoxication can be a defence to a specific intent crime, if it can be proved that the defendant had the required intention, despite his intoxicated state, then the defence will not be available to him. Therefore, **a drunken intent is still an intent**. This is known as the 'dutch courage' concept. Again, this is an example of the courts applying strict guidelines so that people cannot use intoxication as an excuse for criminal behaviour.

CASE: _Attorney General for Northern Ireland v Gallagher (1963)_ – the defendant bought a knife to kill his wife, and a bottle of whisky. Before committing the offence, he drunk the whisky and used the knife to stab her. His conviction for murder was upheld, because the court was satisfied that he still possessed the required intention for murder.

Involuntary intoxication

Involuntary intoxication is where the defendant becomes intoxicated through no fault or knowledge of his own. Here, it will be a complete defence so long as it is proved that the defendant lacked the *mens rea* to commit the offence. This is regardless of the type of offence, because if he has no *mens rea* then he cannot form the intention to commit a specific intent offence and because he has become involuntarily intoxicated, he has not been reckless in becoming intoxicated and has therefore not formed the *mens rea* for a basic intent offence.

Laced drinks:

CASE: *R v Kingston (1994)* – the defendant, who had a history of irresistible urges towards young boys, had his coffee drugged by someone wanting to blackmail him. He was then shown a sleeping 15-year-old boy and was invited to abuse him. The blackmailer photographed him committing indecent assault. The House of Lords upheld the conviction because the defendant would have formed the required *mens rea* for the offence, despite his intoxicated state.

Unknown side effects from prescribed drugs:

CASE: *R v Hardie (1985)* – the defendant took Valium that had been prescribed to his girlfriend, in order to calm him down after the relationship broke down. He then set fire to the living room where his ex-girlfriend and daughter were residing. The court accepted that this was not a usual side effect to what is normally a sedative drug, so therefore Hardie could use the defence of intoxication.

Self defence

There are essentially two defences that fall under this heading, one based in the common law and one that has its origins in statute.

COMMON LAW where a person uses violence in order to protect themselves or another.

STATUTE *s.3 Criminal Law Act 1967* – where a person uses reasonable force to prevent the commission of a crime or to carry out a lawful arrest.

Further guidance for these defences has been provided under *s.76 Criminal Justice and Immigration Act 2008*. This does not change the law, but merely provides guidance on the elements of the defence.

Both defences have the same criteria and can be used together, for example where a householder defends himself against an intruder, he can rely on the common law defence because he was protecting himself, but also the statutory defence because he was preventing the crime of burglary being committed against his property.

The case of *R v Anthony Martin (2001)* attracted huge media attention because Mr Martin was a farmer who was imprisoned for the murder of an intruder to his property. This raised much controversy as to how far a householder is permitted to use reasonable force to protect their homes. In June 2011, Justice Secretary Ken Clarke promised that the law on defending one's property will be clarified. He has hinted that a householder will be able to use 'whatever force is necessary to protect their home' under new legislation. Do you think that this is an appropriate definition?

Research the following cases, also involving householders defending their property:

- *Peter Flanagan (2011)*
- *Munir Hussain (2010)*
- *David Fullard (2009)*.

Think about the shooting of *Jean Charles de Menezes* in 2005 – here the police mistook Menezes for a suicide bomber. No police officers have been prosecuted for this crime as the court accepted the facts as the police believed them to be at the time. Do you agree with this approach, or should public services such as the police be subject to different guidelines?

Grade boost

Notwithstanding the case concerning *Anthony Martin*, between 1990 and 2005, the Crown Prosecution Service brought just 11 prosecutions against householders who had defended their property against burglars. This suggests that the law is on the side of the defendant who uses reasonable force.

Necessary – This means that a defendant can only use the defence if his actions were necessary in the circumstances, that is because there is a threat of harm to himself or someone else, or necessary in the prevention of a crime being committed.

Did the defendant have an opportunity to retreat?	This has become less relevant now since the case of *R v McInnes (1971)*, where the court suggested that if the defendant did have an opportunity to retreat from the threat, this may be evidence to the jury that the force was not necessary or indeed reasonable.
Was the threat imminent?	This means that the threat must be immediate. The defendant need not wait to be hit first, but there must be an element of urgency and inevitability. **CASE: *Attorney General's Reference (No. 2 of 1983)*** – there had been extreme rioting in a particular area and a shopkeeper made up and stored petrol bombs in readiness for defending his property if required. The court held that there was a sufficient imminence to the threat to justify the defence. **CASE: *Malnik v DPP (1989)*** – the court held in this case that carrying a weapon to a person's house who has a violent history was not a sufficiently imminent threat as the defendant had voluntarily put himself in the position to be attacked.
If a mistake was made as to the extent of the threat, the court will look at what the defendant **believed it to be at the time**.	*s.76(4) Criminal Justice and Immigration Act 2008* confirmed the situation and suggested that the belief of the threat has to be **reasonable**. **CASE: *R v Williams (Gladstone) (1987)*** – if the defendant makes a mistake and believes he is under attack when he is not, he is judged in the facts as he saw them so long as the mistake was genuinely made and reasonable under the circumstances.

Reasonable – What constitutes reasonable force is a matter for the jury to decide; a balance must be sought between the force used and the threat that was being prevented.

Was the force used reasonable?	In the case of *R v McInnes (1971)*, the court suggested that if the defendant did have an opportunity to retreat from the threat, this may be evidence to the jury that the force was not necessary or indeed reasonable. *s.76(6) Criminal Justice and Immigration Act 2008* suggests that the reasonable force has to be proportionate to the threat. **CASE: *Cross v Kirkby (2000)*** – here the court maintained that 'reasonable' could include as much as 25% more force being used than necessary. In the case, a farmer was defending his land during an anti-hunt demonstration. One of the protesters hit the farmer in the arm with a baseball bat, and the farmer retaliated by cracking the protester's skull, causing permanent damage. The court is quite lenient in terms of accepting the fact that the defendant is acting in the heat of the moment, and so allows for the fact that they cannot make precise calculations. Thus, in *Attorney General for Northern Ireland's Reference (No. 1 of 1975) (1977)*, the court held that it must be taken into account the limited amount of time for reflection and reaction.

If a mistake was made as to the degree of force needed in a situation, the court will look at it objectively, that is whether they **actually** used reasonable force, not whether they **believe** they used reasonable force.

s.76(3) Criminal Justice and Immigration Act 2008 stipulates that it must be an objective test, and the mistake of the defendant cannot be taken into account.

Here, we must revisit the case of *R v Anthony Martin (2001)*, where the defendant did indeed use the amount of force he thought necessary at the time to defend his property. However, he made a mistake about the amount of force he was entitled to use. He shot the intruder three times, including once in the back. Shooting the intruder in the back suggested that the threat was no longer imminent as the intruder was walking away. This led to him being convicted of murder, though this was later reduced to manslaughter on the grounds of diminished responsibility.

Duress

This is where a person is forced to commit a crime because they were under threat of death or personal injury by another. It is the classic 'do this or else' situation, and can be brought about by a direct threat or circumstances. It often applies to situations concerning gangs or other organised crime agencies.

Duress by threats

There is a two-part test which needs to be passed in order to rely on this defence, and the test seeks to address the balance between the seriousness of the threat and the seriousness of the resulting criminal behaviour.

R v Graham (1982) put into place the two-part test, but restrictions have been put into place by the more recent case of *R v Hasan (2005)*.

Part 1 – Subjective test

Was the defendant forced to act as he did because he feared that otherwise death or personal injury would result to the defendant or to someone for whom the defendant reasonably regarded himself as responsible?

Are the threats sufficiently serious?	Only threats of death or personal injury will be regarded as sufficiently serious to constitute duress.
	CASE: *R v Valderrama-Vega (1985)* – in this case the defendant took part in the illegal importation of drugs from Colombia. He said that he was acting as part of a Mafia type group who had threatened to kill him and expose his homosexuality if he did not take part in the crime.
	CASE: *R v Hasan (2005)* – the court confirmed the position that there must be threat of death or serious personal injury.

R v Graham (1982) – the defendant was a homosexual living with his wife and his lover, King, who had violent tendencies. Threatened by King, the defendant strangled his wife with electrical flex. The defence of duress failed because the court did not believe any threat existed.

R v Hasan (2005) – here the defendant had associations with a drug dealer. The dealer told the defendant to burgle a house and steal money. If he did not comply, the dealer told the defendant that his family would be harmed. He could not rely on the defence because he voluntarily associated himself with these criminal 'gangs'.

stretch&challenge

In relation to the subjective test that the threats to the defendant must be unavoidable, research the following cases and discuss whether the threat was regarded by the courts as 'unavoidable':

R v Hudson and Taylor (1971)

R v Abdul-Hussain (1999)

Do you think these cases would have been decided differently post-*Hasan*?

Are the threats unavoidable?	This part of the test allows for the defendant to have escaped or reported the threat to the police. In other words, the defence will only succeed where the threat is unavoidable and imminent. This was confirmed in *R v Hasan (2005)*. This case showed a serious and strict application of the test, unlike in previous cases where immediate and imminent has been interpreted as the threat posed to a witness in court where a gang member is sat in the public gallery.
The defence is not available to those who have voluntarily self-induced duress.	Once again, *R v Hasan (2005)* has provided guidance and stipulated that the defence of duress is not available where: *'as a result of the accused's voluntary association with others engaged in criminal activity, he foresaw or ought reasonably to have foreseen the risk of being subjected to any compulsion by threats of violence.'*

Part 2 – Objective test

Would a sober person of reasonable firmness, sharing the defendant's characteristics, have reacted to that situation by behaving as the defendant did?

Personal characteristics can only be regarded where they are relevant to the defendant's interpretation of the threat.	The leading case of *R v Bowen (1996)* stipulated when personal characteristics can be taken into account when deciding the actions of the reasonable man. Age and sex – *R v Bowen (1996)* Pregnancy Serious physical disability Recognised mental illness – *R v Martin (2000)*

Duress of circumstances

The rules here are similar to that of duress by threats, but rather than pressure being put on the defendant by another person, the circumstances are such that death or personal injury will ensue if a crime is not committed. The majority of cases in this category are associated with road traffic offences, whereby someone is forced to drive in an illegal manner because of the circumstances.

The test is the same as that of duress by threats; in so much as there is an objective and subjective test which have to be passed.

CASE: *R v Willer (1986)* – here the defendant was charged with reckless driving, but claimed he was forced to drive in such a fashion because he was being chased by a gang of around 30 members. When the gang surrounded the car, he was forced to drive on the pavement in a pedestrian area. It was clear that Willer was being threatened, there was no possibility of him avoiding the threat and anyone in his position would have reacted in the same way.

CASE: *R v Conway (1989)* – Conway was in a car with a passenger who had earlier been in a car in which someone had been shot. On this occasion, the car was being approached by two men, who unknown to the defendant and his passenger were plain clothed police officers. Fearing that they were going to attack the car, the defendant drove off in a reckless manner. Once again, the defence of duress of circumstances was allowed, because from an objective viewpoint, the defendant acted reasonably to avoid a threat of death or serious personal injury.

It is not only road traffic offences which have been held to amount to duress of circumstances; indeed with the exception of murder, the defence is available across all of the criminal law.

Consent

This is where the victim has consented to be injured by the defendant. It is a common law defence, and there is much contrasting case law in the area. The existence of this defence is the recognition that we are free to independently control our lives in any way we see fit.

As a whole, consent can only be used for minor injuries, mainly assault and battery, but there are exceptions which will be explored later, where consent can be used as a defence where more serious harm is inflicted. In order for consent to be successful, there has to be **informed consent** and that informed consent has to cover the **nature and degree of harm** caused to the victim. For more serious harm, the activity has to fall under the accepted public policy exceptions. There has to be a balance between the social usefulness of the activity and the level of harm caused.

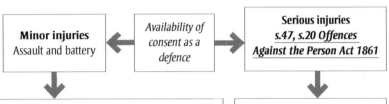

Informed consent

You must be aware to what you are consenting, and the victim has to be made fully aware of the full facts in order to make an informed decision.

CASE: *R v Dica (2004)* – here the defendant knew he was HIV positive, but still continued to have unprotected sexual intercourse. He claimed that his sexual partners impliedly consented to the unprotected sex and thus the risk of HIV infection, but the court rejected this, and held that consent to sexual intercourse was not consent to any injury or infection.

Consent cannot be obtained by fraud as held in the case of *R v Tabassum (2000)* where a rogue doctor examined women's breasts and was convicted of indecent assault.

Nature and degree of harm

This means that the courts will look at the nature and degree of harm consented to by the defendant. The general rule is that the degree of harm accepted is usually very minor, unless the activity is one which falls under the public policy exceptions.

CASE: *R v Brown (1993)* – a group of sadomasochistic homosexuals engaged in consensual sexual activity such as whipping, branding, applying stinging nettles and inserting sharp objects into genitalia. This took place in private with the consent of all the individuals concerned. However, a video of the event was accidentally seen by police and the men were charged with non-fatal offences under **s.47, s.20 Offences Against the Person Act 1861**. This conviction was upheld despite the evidence of consent and lack of permanent damage to the participants.

Activity must be one of public policy or social usefulness:

- Sports
- Rough horseplay
- Tattooing
- Non-violent sexual relations
- Surgery
- Ear piercing
- Male circumcision

stretch & challenge

Research the following cases, all concerning one of the public policy exceptions in relation to consent:

R v Donovan (1934) – sexual activity

R v Boyea (1992) – sexual activity

R v Aitken and others (1992) – horseplay

R v Lloyd (1989) – sports (rugby)

Grade boost

It is a common examination question to ask for an evaluation on the law of consent, and whether or not the defence truly exists in English and Welsh law.

Public policy exceptions

As already mentioned, there are occasions where a defendant can consent to serious injury – this has to be an issue of social usefulness. For example, in the case of *R v Leach (1969)*, the victim had arranged to be crucified and nailed to a wooden cross. The defendants were found liable under *s.18 Offences Against the Person Act 1861* and were not allowed to rely on the victim's consent because the activity was not one which would be regarded as socially beneficial.

Some activities which would be regarded as socially useful are:

Sports

Consent can be used as a defence during sports or games provided the players are acting within the rules of the game. The law stipulates that only force which the game usually requires is allowed; for example, in football it would be permitted to kick another player off the ball.

CASE: *R v Barnes (2004)* – here, the defendant injured the leg of another player during a match. Even though the tackle was late, unnecessary and high and contrary to the rules of the game, the defence of consent was allowed. The judge made it clear that just because a foul has been committed that may result in a player being sent off, that is not enough justification to exclude the defence of consent. The conduct must go outside what is expected during the normal course of a game for the defence to be excluded.

This case can be contrasted:
CASE: *R v Moss (2000)* – in this case, the defendant was convicted because during the course of a rugby match, he punched an opponent in the face, which resulted in a fractured eye socket. He was convicted of an offence under *s.20 Offences Against the Person Act 1861*.

Lawful surgery

Consent is a defence to lawful surgery since the operation is necessary for the benefit of the patient. This is also the case for ritual operations, such as circumcision for religious purposes, as seen in the case of *Re J (Prohibited steps order: circumcision) (1999)*.

Since the case of *Gillick v West Norfolk Area Health Authority (1986)*, parents are able to consent on behalf of their children until such a time as they become **Gillick competent** to make the decision for themselves.

Tattooing and body piercing

Statute provides for this to be consented to, over the age of 18, although this is a relatively recent change in the law.

CASE: *Burrell v Harmer (1967)* – the defendants caused actual bodily harm to the victims by tattooing them when they were aged just 12 and 13. The defendant was convicted as the victims did not appreciate the nature of the act to which they were consenting. Post-*Gillick*, they would have been regarded as not **Gillick competent**.

CASE: *R v Wilson (Alan) (1996)* – this was a case where Wilson had, at the request and with the consent of his wife, branded his initials on her buttocks. He was charged with an offence under *s.47 Offences Against the Person Act 1861*, but his appeal was allowed with the Court of Appeal confirming that such consensual, non-aggressive behaviour fell within the realms of tattooing and thus formed a recognised exception to the rule laid out in *R v Brown (1993)*.

Non-violent sexual relations

The law allows for vigorous sexual activity so long as there was no intention to cause injury, and that the activity was consensual.

CASE: *R v Slingsby (1995)* – the victim died from septicaemia when the defendant penetrated her with his hand causing her internal cuts from a signet ring he was wearing. She did not realise the severity of her injuries and died when the cuts went septic.

The court has distinguished between injuries caused by sexual activity which is intentional (*R v Brown (1996)*) and that which is purely reckless (*R v Slingsby (1995)*) in deciding whether the defence of consent will be available.

Rough horseplay

This is a contentious issue because here the law allows for the defence of consent for rough horseplay, but it may be perceived by some as bullying, though the courts do seem to have insisted on a lack of intention to cause injury.

CASE: *R v Jones (1986)* – the victim who died suffered serious injuries from a ruptured spleen during 'birthday bumps' when the defendant and others threw him in the air. There was no intention to cause the harm, so the schoolboys could rely on the defence of consent.

Evaluation of defences

Insanity/Automatism

- **Definition** – The definition of insanity comes from the very old case of *M'Naghten (1843)*, rather than from medically recognised illnesses, therefore there is a huge social stigma attached to this and people will have the label of 'insane' when they sleepwalk or have medically controlled diseases such as epilepsy or diabetes.

- **Sentencing** – The court has disposals available when sentencing, which include committal to a mental institution. This seems a little harsh for someone who is not regarded as medically insane or even suffering from a medically recognised disease.

- **Absurd application** – There have been cases where the definition has been applied absurdly – for example, in the contrasting cases of *R v Quick (1973)* and *R v Hennessey (1989)*, it would seem that the defence of insanity applies in cases of diabetics where the defendant DID NOT take their insulin, but is not available in cases where diabetics HAVE taken their insulin.

- **Narrow application** – The definition of insanity can be rather narrow, and some defendants who are actually medically deemed to be insane do not fall within the legal definition and so the defence is not available. This happened in *R v G and J (2008)* where the defendants were prosecuted for terrorism offences. Medical evidence showed that he was psychotic and was responding to voices in his head. The House of Lords held that he was not 'legally' insane and so therefore could not rely on the defence. This was also the case in *R v Byrne (1960)*.

Grade boost

It is a common examination question, particularly on LA4, to be asked to evaluate one or more defences. It is important when answering these questions that, as well as being able to describe the defence and its availability, you are able to provide some evaluation as to the criticisms of the defence.

Grade boost

You should show knowledge of reforms where necessary. In terms of insanity, there have been a few proposals:

- The *Butler Committee* recommended a new defence which would find the defendant 'not guilty on evidence of a mental disorder', which avoids the socially stigmatic label of 'insane'.
- Abolition of the rules laid out in **M'Naghten**, or at least amendment so that they coincide with the current medical guidelines.
- Treating diseases that can be controlled by drugs; that is, diabetes, epilepsy under the defence of automatism.

Grade boost

You should show knowledge of reforms where necessary. In terms of intoxication, there have been a few proposals:

- The *Law Commission* in 1993 recommended a new defence of 'dangerous intoxication', where the maximum sentence would be one year imprisonment for the first offence. This abolishes the need for using lesser offences and the need for the distinction between specific and basic intent offences.
- It has also been suggested that a special verdict be created, whereby the defendant would be found guilty and subject to the normal penalty for that offence, but the intoxication would be taken into account by the judge when sentencing.

- **Burden of proof** – When raising the defence of insanity, the burden of proof is on the defendant to prove that he is insane. There are implications here that this is a breach of **Article 6 ECHR** which guarantees the right to a fair trial, as it is also against the fundamental principle that everyone is innocent until proven guilty.

- **Social stigma** – There is also the argument that the word 'insanity' suggests someone who is a danger to the public. There is nothing dangerous about a diabetic or an epileptic whose illnesses can be controlled by medication and who invariably lead very ordinary lives.

- **Increase in guilty pleas** – Although not a direct criticism, it has been found that more defendants plead guilty to an offence because life imprisonment is preferable to being committed to a mental institution which would be the outcome if they pleaded insanity.

- **Moral dilemma** – Following *R v Windle (1952)*, it would seem that a person can use the defence of insanity if he knew his act was **legally** wrong, but did not know that it was **morally** wrong.

Intoxication

- ***Mens rea* of recklessness?** – It is a basic rule of criminal law that the *actus reus* and the *mens rea* of a crime must coincide – that is, happen simultaneously. However, the decision in ***DPP v Majewski (1977)*** suggested that becoming intoxicated was a reckless course of conduct and enough to satisfy the *mens rea* of a basic intent offence. This is contrary to that basic rule, because a defendant will often become intoxicated hours before committing the *actus reus* of a crime. This means that a defendant has committed 'half a crime' just by becoming intoxicated with no idea that they may commit an offence.

- **Lesser offences** – For some crime, such as theft, there is no lesser offence, so where a defendant was intoxicated for a specific intent crime, that has no basic intent equivalent, he will be charged with no offence.

- **Unfair application** – Where the defendant has become involuntarily intoxicated, he can still be found guilty if it can be proved he formed the required *mens rea* – such as in the case of ***R v Kingston (1993)***. It can be argued that this is an unfair application of the law.

- **Public policy** – There needs to be a balance between protecting victims and allowing the defence on the grounds of public policy. A huge number of crimes are committed by defendants who are intoxicated, and the point needs to be made clear that intoxication cannot be used as an excuse for criminal behaviour.

- **Purposeful intoxication?** – The law makes no distinction between defendants who get drunk with the sole purpose of committing a crime and those who merely have a few drinks and inadvertently become intoxicated.

- **Jury guidance** – In the case of ***R v Lipman (1970)*** and ***R v Richardson and Irwin (1999)***, the jury were asked to consider whether the defendant would have had the *mens rea* for the offence if he were sober. This is a very difficult task for the jury who are supposed to judge on facts, not on suppositions.

Self defence

- **Householders protecting property** – The biggest criticism of this defence is the controversy surrounding householders who are protecting their property, and the amount of force that can be used to fend off intruders, as seen in the case of *Martin (2002)*.

- **Use of excessive force** – Where the defendant uses excessive force, the defence cannot be used. However, there have been suggestions that the jury should consider that 'some' of the force used was lawful, and that this should be taken into account in subsequent sentencing. This has been highlighted since the case of *R v Clegg (1995)*.

- **Mistaken belief** – The law is lenient on people who make a mistake, but who honestly believe they are at risk. It has been argued that this is potentially contrary to *Article 2 ECHR* which guarantees a right to life. There is also the provision within *Article 2 ECHR* that requires a criminal sanction where someone has killed on the basis of an unreasonable belief.

- **Sex discrimination?** – Most defendants who use this defence are male as they are mainly concerned with non-fatal offences against each other. Female defendants are often the victim of domestic violence and these often go unreported. It is also thought that women are more likely to use a weapon in self defence, and therefore put themselves at risk of having used excessive force.

- **Degree of force** – The clarification of the law as a result of the *Criminal Justice and Immigration Act 2008* means that the degree of force that is relevant has to be reasonable in the circumstances, but the reasonableness is judged against what the defendant believed the circumstances to be.

Consent

- **Sex police?** – Cases such as *R v Brown (1993)* and the contrasting case of *R v Wilson (1996)* have led to controversy because it is thought that the courts should not be responsible for policing sexual relations between consenting adults.

- **Discrimination?** – One big difference between the two cases mentioned above is that in *R v Brown (1993)*, the participants were homosexual, whereas in *R v Wilson (1996)*, the defendants were heterosexual. This has led to speculation that there is some discrimination between sadomasochistic activities conducted between homosexual and heterosexual couples.

- **Inconsistent application** – Research conducted by Feldman (1993) suggested that to allow horseplay, or bullying as it was perceived in *R v Jones (1986)* is inconsistent since those who partake in consensual sexual relations cannot use consent as a defence.

- **Narrow application** – Consent can only be used as a defence to assault or battery. It has therefore been suggested that the defence should be allowed for *s.47 Offences Against the Person Act 1861* since one of the key elements of *s.47* is proof of either assault or battery.

- **Euthanasia** – The continuing euthanasia debate raises criticism on the lack of availability of the defence for assisting people to die. There is obviously a danger that this defence could be abused, were it allowed, such as in the case of *Harold Shipman*, who killed more than fifteen of his patients whilst working as a GP. However, on the other hand, cases such as *Diane Pretty* and *Diane Purdy* highlight how consent as a defence would be appropriate.

stretch&challenge

Look up the case of *R v Clegg (1995)* – this case involved a soldier who killed a passenger in a car which passed through his checkpoint. The fatal shot was the fourth shot, which Clegg shot to the back of the head of the victim, and this was held to be excessive force. This attracted huge media interest and resulted in Clegg's early release. Do you think the public services should be locked up for 'doing their job'? Research similar cases where the public services have been held to account for their actions; do you agree with the outcomes? What are the arguments for imprisoning them?

stretch&challenge

Revisit the case of *Jean Charles de Menezes* – do you think the police held an unreasonable belief when they shot him?

stretch&challenge

In a Sunday Times survey 60% of doctors agreed that they should have the power to assist death without fear of prosecution. Research the following cases and discuss what approach is generally taken to doctors and health care professionals who assist their patients to die?

- *Rachael Heath (1996)*
- *Dr David Moor (1999)*
- *Dr Cox (1992)*

Grade boost

The Law Commission, in 1977, proposed to abolish the defence of duress. Some of their arguments against the defence include:

- Doing wrong can never be justified.
- Willingness to rely on duress as the motive for committing a crime.
- The defence helps gang crime, terrorists and other criminal groups.

Key terminology

Presumption = a presumption is a starting point for the courts. They presume certain facts to be true unless there is a greater preponderance of evidence to the contrary that rebuts the presumption.

Synoptic link

Judges use statutory interpretation to interpret statutes to determine if Parliament intended the offence to be one of strict liability. This is an AS level topic and is covered in the *WJEC AS Law: Study and Revision Guide*. There is a clear synoptic link with strict liability as judges have to use aids of interpretation, such as the literal, golden, mischief and purposive approaches, to determine if an offence was intended to be one of strict liability. They also have to use rules of language and the presumption that *mens rea* is required.

Duress

- **Too narrow** – There is the criticism that the case of **_R v Hasan (2005)_** put too many restrictions on the defence because it was being relied upon by members of gangs and those who were involved in criminal activity by choice. It has been suggested that the objective element of the defence is unnecessary since it punishes anyone who is associated with a criminal. Further, it has been suggested that the female victim of domestic violence who has been bullied into committing a crime may be denied the defence, since they would be regarded as having 'self-induced' the duress.
- **Use for murder?** – Duress is not permitted for the offence of murder, and this is seen as harsh particularly in light of the terrorist climate in which we find ourselves, where people are forced and coerced into committing crimes because of the threat to themselves or their families.

Strict Liability Offences

Components of a strict liability offence

Most crimes require both *actus reus* and *mens rea*. However, there is a group of offences known as **strict liability** where only the *actus reus* needs to be proved in order to establish liability. With these offences, there is no need to prove *mens rea* for at least one element of the *actus reus* and liability is imposed without fault on the part of the defendant. As a result of this, some feel strict liability offences are unfair, but, as they cover relatively minor crimes, it is generally accepted that they are needed to allow society to run smoothly. They tend to cover regulatory offences such as food hygiene, parking offences and polluting the environment. For strict liability offences, the defence of mistake is not available.

There is also a group of crimes known as **absolute liability** offences. These offences require proof of *actus reus* only but are not concerned with whether or not the *actus reus* is voluntary. The chapter on 'Elements of Crime' refers to these offences as 'state of affairs' crimes and demonstrates through the cases of **_Winzar_** and **_Larsonneur_** that the *actus reus* need not be controlled by the defendant.

Though the majority of strict liability offences are statutory offences, Parliament does not always make it clear whether or not *mens rea* is required. It is therefore for judges to decide whether an offence should be one of strict liability or not. Judges start with the **presumption** that ***mens rea* is always required** and no offence is strict liability. They then consider four factors to confirm or rebut this presumption. The case of **_Gammon (HK) Ltd v Attorney General (1985)_**, where builders had failed to follow exact plans and part of the building collapsed, confirmed that the starting point for a judge is to presume that *mens rea* is always required before a person can be found guilty of a criminal offence.

A key case demonstrating the application of strict liability is **_Pharmaceutical Society of Great Britain v Storkwain Ltd (1986)_**.

The four factors

1. Is the offence regulatory in nature or a true crime?

If the offence is regulatory in nature (meaning not really criminal, minor, no moral issue involved), the offence is more likely to be classed as strict liability. A case that considered this question is **Sweet v Parsley (1970)**. In this case, Ms Sweet sublet her property to a group of tenants, retaining a room for herself but hardly spending any time there. The police searched the property and found cannabis. Ms Sweet was convicted under **s.5 Dangerous Drugs Act 1965** (now replaced), of 'being concerned in the management of premises used for the smoking of cannabis'. She appealed, alleging that she had no knowledge of the circumstances and indeed could not have reasonably been expected to have such knowledge. On appeal, her conviction was overturned with Lord Reid acknowledging that strict liability was only appropriate for 'quasi-crimes' where no real moral issue was involved. Ms Sweet's conviction had caused her to lose her job and had damaged her reputation. It was felt that strict liability was inappropriate and the offence should be classed as a 'true crime' requiring *mens rea*. She did not have any *mens rea* so her conviction was quashed.

Key case

In the case of **Cundy v Le Cocq (1884)**, the defendant was convicted of unlawfully selling alcohol to an intoxicated person, contrary to **s.13 Licensing Act 1872**. It was held that it was not necessary to consider whether the defendant knew, should have known or should have used reasonable care to detect that the person was intoxicated. As soon as the defendant sold the alcohol to the drunken person, he was guilty of the offence.

2. Does the offence relate to an issue of social concern?

An issue of social concern is something that is of concern to general society at a given time. Issues of social concern can shift over time but tend to relate to offences such as selling alcohol or cigarettes to minors, pollution and public safety. By imposing strict liability for crimes that relate to issues of social concern, it is felt that this will promote extra vigilance and care on the part of defendants to not commit the offence. Of course, this is only appropriate for regulatory offences and the distinction drawn in the **Sweet v Parsley** case is still applicable.

In the case of **Harrow London Borough Council v Shah (1999)** the defendants were convicted of selling National Lottery tickets to a child under 16. It did not matter that they believed the child to be over 16, the offence was committed as soon as they had sold the lottery ticket to a person under 16. The courts felt this offence related to an issue of social concern.

Synoptic link

With this factor, consider the impact of statutory interpretation and precedent from AS Level Law. What are the different ways that judges *interpret statutes* and if a judge in, for example, the Court of Appeal takes a certain interpretation of a word, how will this set a *precedent* for future similar cases?

3. Did Parliament intend to create an offence of strict liability by using certain words in a statute?

There are some words that Parliament uses when drafting statutes that point to *mens rea* being required. '*Mens rea* words' include: *intentionally*, *recklessly* and *knowingly*. Though there is no official list of words that point towards a crime being one of strict liability, there are some that have generally been interpreted by judges as pointing towards no *mens rea* being required. These include: *possession* and *cause*.

In the case of **Alphacell v Woodward (1972)** the defendants were charged with *causing* polluted matter to enter a river. The pumps that prevented the pollution from overflowing into the river had become clogged with leaves and as a result the matter leaked into the river. It was irrelevant that the defendants had no idea the pumps were clogged with leaves and had not wanted any contamination to enter the river. They had *caused* the polluted matter to enter the river and were therefore liable.

Grade boost

Though punishments are usually small for strict liability offences, the case of *Gammon* is an exception. In this case the penalty was a fine of up to $250,000 or three years' imprisonment.

stretch&challenge

Many of the cases in this unit overlap to demonstrate more than one factor. For example. the *Alphacell* case can be used to show how some words indicate strict liability was intended by Parliament but also an issue of social concern (pollution). Think about the other cases in this unit and how they may demonstrate more than one of the factors.

Key terminology

Deterrent = something that discourages a particular action.

Grade boost

Think of cases to demonstrate the ways that courts have protected society through the imposition of strict liability. Use these cases to provide the evaluation required for higher marks. For example:

Sale of unfit meat: ***Callow v Tillstone***

Pollution: ***Alphacell v Woodward***

Dangerous buildings: ***Gammon***

Food hygiene: ***Callow v Tillstone***

stretch&challenge

Deterrence is also linked to theories of punishment later in this study guide. A harsh sentence is more likely to be a deterrent from committing crime.

stretch&challenge

Explore the following cases and consider how the question of strict liability in relation to Human Rights was dealt with by the courts:

Hansen v Denmark (1995)

Salabiaku v France (1988)

4. The gravity of the punishment

The more serious the criminal offence and punishment that can be imposed, the less likely it is to be one of strict liability. This reflects the fact that with strict liability, defendants can be convicted without fault. As will be considered below, this can be problematic as the small penalties do not always act as a deterrent. On the other hand, as in the case of ***Callow v Tillstone (1900)*** the damage to a small business's reputation can be far greater than the impact of a small fine. In this case, a butcher was convicted of 'exposing unfit meat for sale'. The butcher was found guilty even though he had taken reasonable care not to commit the offence by having the carcass inspected by a vet who said it was ok to eat.

Advantages and disadvantages of strict liability

Advantages	Disadvantages
▪ **Time and cost of proving *mens rea*** *Mens rea* can be difficult to prove and if it had to be proved for every offence, the courts would be rather clogged with cases and some guilty individuals may escape conviction. This in turn would increase court costs.	▪ **Possibility of injustice** The main criticism of strict liability is that liability is imposed without fault on the part of the defendant. Individuals may have taken all reasonable steps to avoid the behaviour and be unaware they are committing the illegal act yet still face conviction. The injustice is magnified further with absolute liability offences as in the case of ***Larsonneur***.
▪ **Protection of society by promoting a higher standard of care** As strict liability offences are so easy to prove, individuals may take more care when acting in certain situations thereby protecting society from harmful behaviour.	▪ **Role of judges** Judges are interpreting what they think Parliament intended by an Act. This gives judges an increased role and there is a risk of inconsistency in the imposition of strict liability.
▪ **The ease of imposing strict liability acts as a deterrent** Individuals are deterred from carrying out the offending behaviour in the knowledge that a prosecution is likely to result in a conviction due to only having to prove the *actus reus*.	▪ **Is strict liability actually a deterrent?** As a result of the small penalties imposed for strict liability, some argue that it does not act as a deterrent. Larger businesses may continue to carry out the offending behaviour, paying the small fines and not change their practices. In addition, to act as a deterrent it is argued that a person ought to have knowledge that what they are doing is wrong in order to take steps to prevent it. This is not always the case with strict liability offences.
▪ **Proportionality of the punishment appropriate for strict liability** As discussed above, strict liability offences tend to carry small penalties. This is appropriate since defendants may be unaware they are committing the offence or have taken all reasonable steps to avoid doing so.	▪ **Does strict liability breach the European Convention on Human Rights?** There has been some debate over whether the strict liability infringes the European Convention on Human Rights. According to article 6(2) of the ECHR, everyone should be presumed innocent until proven guilty according to law. The most recent case: ***R v G (2008)*** appears to allow the imposition of strict liability.

Proposal for reform

The Law Commission had previously proposed a **Criminal Liability (Mental Element) Bill (1977)** (not enacted) where the onus would be on Parliament, if it wished to create an offence of strict liability, to make this clear in the Act of Parliament. It is Parliament's responsibility to decide the nature of criminal liability and to provide a clear indication to judges whether it intended to create a crime with no requirement of *mens rea*. This would prevent some of the confusion and inconsistency of judicial decisions.

Sentencing

Theories of sentencing

Types of sentencing

A sentence is the punishment given to the defendant when they are convicted, and the type of sentence can vary depending on whether the defendant is an adult or youth offender. The sentence that can be given to an offender depends on the government of the time and their priorities, which are often affected by current events and media pressure.

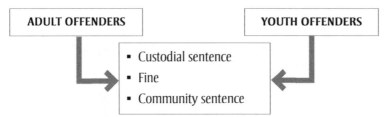

Both adult and youth offenders can receive the same type of sentence, but they vary in terms of their requirements and their length.

The judge is responsible for sentencing in both the Crown Court and the Magistrates' Court. The range of sentences available to each court does vary:

MAGISTRATE'S COURT
- £5,000 fine
- 6 months in prison (12 months for consecutive sentences)
- Youth Detention and Training Order for up to two years

CROWN COURT
- Unlimited fine
- Life imprisonment

The **tariff** or length of the sentence will be determined by the court, which will look at the following factors:
- The age of the offender.
- The seriousness of the offence.
- The likelihood of further offences being committed.
- The extent of harm likely to result from further offences.

stretch&challenge

1. Look at the different types of sentencing, and discuss which theory you think they support.

2. The government has recently published a Consultation Document entitled, 'More Effective Responses to Anti-Social Behaviour' which contains proposals for the abolition of Anti-Social Behaviour Orders (ASBOs) and replacing them with two new measures to prevent anti-social behaviour. These include: Criminal Behaviour Order – this will have the effect of banning the defendant from certain activities or places. Community Protection Order – this deals with place-related anti-social behaviour and will impose restrictions on the use of places which act as a magnet for criminal behaviour.

Extension

Research the new powers given to police under these proposals – do you think these Orders and the new powers are an effective way of dealing with anti-social behaviour?

Aims of sentencing

Aims of sentencing for adult offenders are laid out in **s.142 Criminal Justice Act 2003**. It is often the case that people assume the one aim of sentencing is to punish individuals, but other factors need to be taken into consideration, such as the effect on the community and the long-term rehabilitation of the offender.

Retribution (punishment)

This is the classic aim of sentencing, and is a way of punishing the defendant because it has been established that he has committed a crime and an element of blame rests with him. The punishment must fit the crime, and so the sentence given must be proportionate to the crime that has been committed.

Deterrence

Individual deterrence – this is where the individual offender is deterred from offending again.

General deterrence – this is aimed at deterring others from committing a crime, showing society the potential consequences of committing a crime and making an example of the offender.

Obviously the harsher the sentence, the more likely it is to act as a deterrent.

Protection of society

This is where the sentence given to an offender is one which will protect the public from the offender. For example, a dangerous driver could be given a ban, or a convicted burglar could be given an electronic tag to keep him from being out of the house after dark.

Rehabilitation

This is where the offender is given a sentence which will help rehabilitate his behaviour and prevent him from offending again. This is particularly effective for Youth Offenders where it seems to be widely agreed that a period of imprisonment is not effective in preventing re-offending. It is for this reason that the Criminal Justice Act 2003 offers Community Sentencing which can be tailored with requirements to help the offender and the community as a whole.

Reparation

Reparation essentially means paying back to society what you have taken away – this can be in the form of compensation, or through the completion of unpaid community work. For example, someone who has been convicted of criminal damage may be ordered to remove all the graffiti or repair any damage that has been caused.

Youth offenders

Offenders aged between 10 and 17 are classed as youth offenders, and are usually tried in the **Youth Court**, except where the case is very serious, and in such circumstances will be tried in the Crown Court. Youths can also be tried in the Crown Court if they are being tried alongside an adult offender. The role of the Youth Court was consolidated in the case of *Thompson and Venables v UK (1999)* where the ECHR held that it was a breach of *Article 6 ECHR* to have youths tried in an adult court because it was perceived as intimidating and daunting for them.

The Youth Court is usually located in the same building as the Magistrates' Court. It is not open to the public and is more informal in terms of the fact that the District Judges do not wear wigs and there is only limited access for the press. Young offenders are also entitled to have an **appropriate adult** with them at all times, and this is provided for under *s.57 Police and Criminal Evidence Act 1984* and *Code C*.

There are several different types of sentences available for youths, but the primary aim of youth sentencing, according to *s.142 Criminal Justice Act 2003* is to prevent re-offending and rehabilitate the offender to change their behaviour whilst compensating or 'repairing' society for the damage that has been caused.

PRE-COURT SENTENCING
These are disposals available in the youth justice system for those offenders who have committed a first offence or who plead guilty to an offence

Police Reprimand
This is a formal warning given by a police officer to a youth who has admitted committing an offence or who has been caught committing an offence. The offence must be a minor first offence, and the youth will be given the opportunity to voluntarily partake in a programme run by the **Youth Offending Team** which will address their behaviour.

Final warning
This is similar to a Reprimand but is given for a second minor offence, to which the youth pleads guilty. The Youth Offending Team programme will become compulsory in this instance, and a programme of activities will be written to address the offending behaviour.

YOUTH REHABILITATION ORDER
These were introduced under *ss1-4 Criminal Justice and Immigration Act 2008*

It is a type of community sentence that replaced nine previous sentences. It is a flexible Order which has the overall aim of reducing reoffending and the number of youths in custody. The Order can last for a maximum of three years and can be applied to any criminal offence that has been committed by an individual under the age of 18. The following requirements can be attached to a Youth Rehabilitation Order:

Activity Requirement	*Unpaid Work Requirement*
Curfew Requirement	*Prohibited Activity Requirement*
Exclusion Requirement	*Electronic Monitoring Requirement*
Local Authority Residence Requirement	*Supervision Requirement*
Education Requirement	*Intoxicating Substance Requirement*
Mental Health Treatment Requirement	*Drug Testing Requirement*

Supervision of the youth will be carried out by the **Youth Offending Team**, and the youth will be required to visit with his case worker who will work out a plan with him called a **Youth Rehabilitation Order Plan**, which will address the behaviour and help the young person move forward. If a youth offender breaches their Order three times, they will have to return to court and could face a period in custody.

Grade boost

A common examination question is to ask about the theories of sentencing. When you are talking about each theory, you should give examples of types of sentences that support that theory.

Visit **www.homeoffice.gov. uk/police/powers** where you will find further information on youth sentencing – do you think out of court disposals such as PNDs, Reprimands, Final Warnings and so on are effective alternatives to court punishments for youth offenders?

FIRST-TIER SENTENCING

These are community sentences which are designed to act as a **deterrent** from committing further crime and a way in which the offender can attempt to rehabilitate and prevent re-offending in the future.

Referral Order
ss16–28 Powers of Criminal Courts (Sentencing) Act 2000

This is given for a first offence, when the offender pleads guilty. The Order means the young person will be referred to a Youth Offender Panel, that will draw up a contract which will last between three and twelve months, and the contract will aim to address the causes of the offending behaviour and give the offender an opportunity to repair the damage that has been caused as a result of the offence.

Reparation Order
ss73–75 Powers of Criminal Courts (Sentencing) Act 2000

This is a sentence which allows the offender to take responsibility for their behaviour and express their remorse to society by repairing the harm caused by the offence. This can involve asking the youth to meet with his victim to directly compensate for his actions, or it can be repairing the damage caused by the offender, for example cleaning up graffiti or undertaking some form of unpaid work.

Penalty Notice for Disorder
Criminal Justice and Police Act 2001

This is a fixed penalty which is given to youths who have committed minor crimes, such as theft from shops, minor criminal damage, dropping litter and drunkenness. There are 23 offences altogether for which it can be given.

They are generally given to 16–17 year olds but pilots have been carried out to give them to under 16 year olds.

Once the penalty notice has been served, the young offender must either pay the penalty or elect to go to court.

In 2009, over 11,000 PNDs were issued to 16–17 year olds.

Conditional discharge
ss12–15 Powers of Criminal Courts (Sentencing) Act 2000

This sentence is rarely used, but is a way of giving the offender a 'cooling off' period – the youth will receive no punishment on the condition that they do not reoffend within the next six months to three years. However, if they do reoffend, then the court will consider another sentence.

Absolute discharge
ss12–15 Powers of Criminal Courts (Sentencing) Act 2000

This is a discharge where an offender is released without punishment and nothing further is done.

CUSTODY

Custody will only be granted to a youth in very serious cases heard in the Crown Court

Detention and Training Order
ss100–106 Powers of Criminal Courts (Sentencing) Act 2000

This is a period in custody for a youth offender, and the length can vary between **four months** and **two years**.

The first half of the sentence is served in custody, and the second half of the sentence is served in the community under the supervision of the **Youth Offending Team**. During this community element, the offender will have to undertake reparation work and adhere to any targets contained in the **Training and Supervision Plan** which will have been agreed with their Youth Offending Team worker.

These Orders are only given to those youths who are a particularly high risk, or are persistent offenders, or have committed a particularly serious offence, because custody is not always the most appropriate solution for a youth offender. Any breach of the Order at any stage of the process could result in a fine or continued detention in custody.

s.90 Powers of the Criminal Courts (Sentencing) Act 2000

If the conviction is for murder, the court is obliged to set a minimum term to be spent in custody, after which the youth can apply to the **Parole Board** for release. If they are successful, they will be closely supervised indefinitely. This is a sentence that can only be given by the Crown Court.

s.91 Powers of Criminal Courts (Sentencing) Act 2000

This section deals with those youths who have committed offences, for which an adult offender would spend at least 14 years in prison. The length of the sentence can be anywhere up to the adult maximum, which can be up to life imprisonment.

The young offender can be released automatically at the halfway point, and can be released up to a maximum of 135 days early on a **Home Detention Curfew**. The offender, once released, will also be subject to a supervisory licence until their sentence expires. This is a sentence that can only be given by the Crown Court.

Parenting orders

These are Orders given to parents under the *Criminal Justice Act 2003* for up to a year, which will have conditions attached, such as having to attend counselling sessions, and will contain a list of things their offending child must and must not do, for example making sure that they attend school or are at home between certain hours. They are intended to be a support for the parents in helping them to deal with their child's behaviour. If a parent breaches the Order, they can be subject to a fine of up to £1000. The aim of the Order is to prevent re-offending, and it will only be granted if the court is satisfied that it will help in the prevention of further crime.

Adult offenders

Absolute discharge	This is where the court feels that the offender has received enough punishment by going through court and so discharges the offender with no further action needed.	In 2008, 0.7% of offenders received an absolute discharge.
Conditional discharge	This is where the offender will receive no punishment on the condition that they do not reoffend for a specified period.	In 2008, 6% of offenders received a conditional discharge.
Fine	This is the most common sentence given to adults. Fines are mostly administered for minor offences. Magistrates can give a maximum fine of £5000 and the Crown Court has no limit which it can impose.	In 2008, 65% of offenders received a fine.
Suspended Sentence Order	This is where the offender does not go to prison, but has to comply with conditions set out by the court. The suspended period can be between 14 days and one year (or six months in the Magistrates' Court) Breach of the conditions can result in the offender being sent to prison for the remainder of their sentence. The court can attach any of the 12 requirements to the sentence.	In 2008, 3% of offenders received a suspended sentence.
Community Order	A court can impose a Community Order with any number of the requirements contained in the *Criminal Justice Act 2003*. A Community Order encompasses both punishment and reparation to the community.	In 2008, 14% of offenders received a community order.

Key terminology
Home Detention Curfew = an Order given to an offender which allows them to be released from prison early on the condition that they sign a licence to remain at their home or a specified address between certain times. They will have an electronic tag attached to them, which means that if they move from their designated address, the prison service will be alerted and the offender will have to return to prison.

Determinate sentence = the court sets a fixed amount of time the offender has to spend in prison.

Indeterminate sentence = the courts sets a minimum amount of time the offender has to spend in prison.

Parole Board = a body set up under the **Criminal Justice Act 1967** who will hold a number of hearings with an offender to decide whether they can be released from prison after serving a minimum sentence. They complete a risk assessment to determine whether it is safe to release the person back into the community. If they are safe to be released, they will be released on licence with conditions and close supervision.

▲ Grade boost

There are a number of requirements that can be attached to a suspended sentence or a community sentence for an adult offender. These are included in the **Criminal Justice Act 2003** and can include:

- An unpaid work requirement
- An activity requirement
- A programme requirement
- A prohibited activity requirement
- A curfew requirement
- An exclusion requirement
- A residence requirement
- A mental health treatment requirement
- A drug rehabilitation requirement
- Alcohol treatment requirement
- A supervision requirement.

Custodial sentences

This is the most severe sentence available and is for the most serious of offences. **s.152(2) Criminal Justice Act 2003** stipulates that custodial sentences are only available for those offences 'so serious that neither a fine alone nor a community sentence can be justified for the offence'.

Determinate sentence

This is where the court fixes the amount of time an offender has to stay in prison. This is the most common form of custodial sentence, though the length of sentence is usually a maximum as the offender will not always serve this amount of time.

For sentences of more than a year, the offender is likely to only serve half of their sentence and the other half will be served in the community on licence with conditions attached, and under supervision.

Indeterminate sentence

This is where the court will set a minimum period of time that the offender has to serve in prison before they are eligible for early release by the **Parole Board**.

a) Imprisonment for life

This is covered under **s.225 Criminal Justice Act 2003** and suggests that an offender should serve a sentence of imprisonment for life, where:

- The offender is convicted of a serious offence (defined as carrying a maximum sentence of life imprisonment or at least 10 years).
- In the court's opinion the offender poses a significant risk to the public of serious harm by the commission of further specified offences.
- The maximum penalty for the offence is life imprisonment.
- The court considers that the seriousness of the offence, or the offence and one or more associated offences, justifies the imposition of imprisonment for life.

b) Imprisonment for public protection

This is also covered under **s.225 Criminal Justice Act 2003**, and is given to those offenders where:

- The offender is convicted of a serious sexual or violent offence which is punishable by imprisonment for life or a determinate period of 10 years or more.
- In the court's opinion the offender poses a significant risk to the public of serious harm by the commission of further specified offences.
- The offence is punishable with life imprisonment and the court is satisfied that the seriousness of the offence justifies such a sentence.

The offender has a previous conviction for an offence listed in **schedule 15A to the Criminal Justice Act 2003** or the current offence warrants a notional minimum term of at least two years.

Whole life orders

These are extremely rare, and are given to the most serious offenders or persistent offenders. These prisoners can only be released on compassionate grounds with the permission of the Secretary of State. There are currently 41 prisoners serving Whole life orders in England and Wales.

Mandatory life sentence

This is a compulsory sentence that is given to those offenders who have been found guilty of murder. If they are considered for release by the Parole Board then they will be on a licence for the rest of their lives.

Sentencing Council

The Sentencing Council was set up as part of the ***Coroners and Justice Act 2009***, and replaced the Sentencing Guidelines Council with the aim of encouraging transparency and consistency in sentencing.

When deciding what sentence to impose on an offender, there are several factors that are taken into consideration, depending on whether the offender is an adult or a youth.

The judge will then look at any relevant **sentencing guidelines** pertinent to the offence.

YOUTH OFFENDERS	ADULT OFFENDERS
• The main aim of the youth justice system is to prevent offending • The welfare of the child	The five purposes of sentencing

| When deciding the appropriate sentence, the judge shall consider:
• The offender's age
• The seriousness of the offence
• Any **aggravating** factors
• Any **mitigating** factors
• Whether the offender pleaded guilty
• The relevant law | When deciding the appropriate sentence, the judge shall consider:
• The seriousness of the offence
• The offender's previous convictions
• Any **aggravating** factors
• Any **mitigating** factors
• Personal **mitigation**
• Whether the offender pleaded guilty
• The maximum sentence available for the offence |

| The judge will then look at any relevant **sentencing guidelines** pertinent to the offence | The judge will then look at any relevant **sentencing guidelines** pertinent to the offence |

These factors may be relevant in determining the **type of sentence** as well as the length. Each case is decided on the facts of the individual case.

Key terminology

Aggravating factor = a factor relevant to the offence that has the effect of increasing the sentence given to an offender. An example could be if the defendant has previous convictions, or if a weapon was used in the offence.

Mitigating factor = a factor relevant to the offence that has the effect of decreasing the sentence or a reduced charge. An example could be if it was a first offence, or if the defendant pleaded guilty.

stretch&challenge

The government have recently announced proposals to reduce sentences by 50% for those who plead guilty. Research these proposals and discuss the implications this will have on the prison population. Do you think that this supports the retribution theory of sentencing?

Should life mean life? Convicted murderers Jeremy Bamber, Peter Moore and others are to challenge their granting of a whole life order in the European Court of Human Rights on the grounds that it challenges Article 3 ECHR – right to be free from inhuman and degrading treatment. Discuss these implications and whether you agree with the appeal.

Reasonableness = is a tricky concept and depends on what the individual deems reasonable and acceptable. This provides the police with some measure of discretion in the exercise of their powers.

stretch&challenge

s.4 An officer of rank of superintendent or above can authorise in writing the setting up of road checks to see if the vehicle is carrying: a person who has committed an offence other than a road traffic offence, a person who is a witness to such an offence, a person intending to commit such an offence or a person who is unlawfully at large.

s.44 Terrorism Act 2000 allows the Home Secretary to authorise the police to randomly stop and search persons and vehicles without suspicion in the fight against terrorism. The civil liberties pressure group Liberty won a landmark ruling in the European Court of Human Rights in the case of **Gillan and Quinton v UK** where the s.44 power was held to breach art 8 right to a private life. The s.44 power was suspended in July 2010 as part of the coalition government's Counter Terrorism review and clarification was given in the **Protection of Freedoms Act 2012** where Parliament reinstated the requirement to have reasonable suspicion before stop and search is carried out for terrorism-related offences.

Osman v DPP (1999)
officers failed to give their name or station, therefore making the search unlawful.

Police Powers

The main Act governing police powers is the **Police and Criminal Evidence Act 1984 (PACE)**. Within **PACE** and other Acts, police are given discretion with the ways they exercise their powers, and remedies are available for breach of these powers. Codes of Practice run alongside **PACE** and provide guidelines as to the exercise of certain powers. Breach of the Codes cannot give rise to legal action but if there is a 'serious and substantial' breach, it could lead to evidence being excluded.

Note: All sections are from **PACE** unless stated otherwise.

Stop and search of the person and vehicle

s.1 – Police can stop and search persons or vehicles in a public place or place to which public has access provided there are **reasonable** grounds to suspect they will find stolen or prohibited articles.

s.1(3) – **Criminal Justice Act 2003** – extended power to cover stop and search for articles intended to be used in causing criminal damage.

s.1(6) – Police may seize any stolen or prohibited articles.

Code A Gives guidance on 'reasonable suspicion' and states that it should not be based on personal factors such as age, race, religion, gender, previous convictions or general stereotypes.

s.117 – Reasonable force can be use in carrying out the stop and search. This also applies to the arrest.

s.2 – Police officers should identify themselves, the station at which they are based and the grounds for carrying out the search.

s.2(3) – Police officers not in uniform must provide documentary evidence of their ID.

s.2(9) – Suspect can be asked to remove outer coat, jacket and gloves in public. Headgear and footwear can be removed but in private and in presence of an officer of the same sex.

s.3 – A record should be made of the search, stating the grounds and outcome and a copy provided to the suspect unless this is wholly impractical.

s.60 – **Criminal Justice and Public Order Act 1994** If a police officer of or above the rank of inspector reasonably believes that serious violence will take place in an area, he can authorise the stop and search of persons and vehicles to look for dangerous instruments or offensive weapons in that area for up to 24 hours (which can be extended by a further 30 hours if necessary).

Search of premises

Search of premises can be carried out with or without a warrant. Any property can be searched if a person consents to it.

Search with a warrant

The main provisions are found in *s.8 PACE (1984)*. This gives the police the power to apply for a search warrant to a Magistrate who must be satisfied that the police have reasonable grounds to believe that an indictable offence has been committed and that there is material on the premises which is likely to be of substantial value to the investigation of the offence and that the material is likely to be relevant evidence. It must be impractical for the search to be made without a warrant (e.g., because they cannot communicate with the person, they have not consented to entry or they need immediate entry on arrival at the premises).

Search without a warrant

There are four key sections:

s.17 – Police may enter to make an arrest with or without a warrant, capture a person unlawfully at large or to protect people or prevent damage to property.

s.18 – After an arrest for an indictable offence, police can search premises occupied or controlled by the suspect if they reasonably believe there is evidence of the particular offence or other offences on the premises.

s.32 – After an arrest for an indictable offence an officer can enter and search the premises where the person was when arrested or where they were just before being arrested if the officer reasonably suspects there to be evidence relating to the particular offence on the premises.

s.19 – Once lawfully on the premises, the police can seize and retain any relevant evidence.

Code B provides important guidelines as to the exercise of the power to search premises. It provides that search of premises should be carried out at a reasonable time with reasonable force used and showing due consideration and courtesy towards the property and privacy of the occupier(s).

Power of arrest

Arrest can also be carried out with and without a warrant.

Arrest with a warrant – Police must apply to a Magistrate for an arrest warrant. The name and details of the offence should be specified to the police and once granted provides the power to a constable to enter and search premises to make the arrest if required.

Arrest without a warrant – *s.24 PACE* as amended by **s.110** of the *Serious Organised Crime and Police Act 2005.* An arrest without a warrant can be made if a constable has reasonable grounds to believe that a person **is** committing, **has** committed or is **about** to commit an offence **and** importantly, that an arrest is **necessary**.

stretch&challenge

The **Royal Commission on Criminal Procedure (RCCP)** or 'Philips Commission' concluded in 1981 that a balance needed to be reached between 'the interests of the community in bringing offenders to justice and the rights and liberties of persons suspected or accused of crime'. **PACE** was passed following these findings and consolidated police powers into one Act.

It is important that the police enter premises lawfully, as if they do not, any evidence seized may be inadmissible at in the trial.

Though Code B requires police to carry out searches of property respectfully and only using reasonable force, in reality this is not always possible (e.g., with cases that require an element of surprise or where drugs are involved which could be quickly disposed of).

Grade boost

Search and entry of premises doesn't come up in the exam that frequently but that is not to say it will never come up! The wording used in ss.17, 18 and 32 is quite specific, so look out for whether a person has been arrested first or whether the police are going to the property in order to arrest. This will make a difference to which power should be used.

stretch&challenge

Code A also applies to arrest. Reasonable suspicion can never be based on personal factors alone, including race, age, sex, previous convictions and other general stereotypes.

Art 5 of the ECHR provides that everyone has the right to liberty. Arrest interferes with this right and must be exercised lawfully.

stretch&challenge

Suspects have the right to read the Codes of Practice. Code C also deals with conditions of detention. Suspects must be given adequate food, refreshment, sleep, and breaks. The interview room must be adequately lit, heated and ventilated and a suspect must be allowed to sit. Interviews should not exceed 2 hours in length. Persons under the age of 16 should not be kept in police cells.

Grade boost

It is crucial with police powers to accurately refer to the sections of *PACE* or other Acts that provide the police with the power to carry out a particular act or that guide their conduct. In the exam, remember to: **define** the law, **apply** the law to the facts and reach a **conclusion** as to whether the power was correctly used. Even if something has been done correctly, you still need to discuss what law gives them that power.

The ECHR case of ***O'Hara v UK (2000)*** confirmed the two-part test for reasonable suspicion: The officer must have actual suspicion (subjective) *and* there must be reasonable grounds for that suspicion (objective).

Code G deals with the statutory powers of arrest and gives some examples of when it is necessary to arrest.

s.117 – Can use reasonable force to make the arrest.

s.28 – Even if obvious, the suspect must be told in accessible language they are being arrested and the grounds for the arrest.

Code C The suspect must be cautioned on arrest: '*You do not have to say anything. But it may harm your defence if you do not mention when questioned something which you later rely on in Court. Anything you do say may be given in evidence.*'

s.24A PACE as amended by ***SOCPA*** – Provides a power to a person other than a constable to make an arrest without a warrant of anyone who is in the act of committing an indictable offence, or anyone whom he has reasonable grounds for suspecting to be committing an indictable offence. They must have reasonable grounds for believing an arrest is necessary and that it is impracticable for an officer to make the arrest instead.

s.32 – A constable may search an **arrested** person at a place other than a police station, if they have reasonable grounds for believing that the arrested person may present a danger to himself or others, be in possession of evidence or present a danger.

Key terminology

Necessary to arrest = Under s.24, a constable must have:
(i)   Reasonable grounds for suspecting an offence has been/is about to be committed,
(ii)   Reasonable grounds to suspect the defendant is guilty of it and
(iii)   Reasonable grounds for believing it is **necessary to arrest** the person for reasons given in **s.24(5)**. These grounds are:
a)   To enable the name of the person in question to be ascertained (where it is not known or where the constable believes the one provided to be false).
b)   To enable the address of the person in question to be ascertained as in (a).
c)   To prevent the person in question:
  (i)   causing physical injury to himself or any other person;
  (ii)   suffering physical injury;
  (iii) causing loss of or damage to property;
  (iv)   committing an offence against public; or
  (v)   causing an unlawful obstruction of the highway.
d)   To protect a child or other vulnerable person from the person in question.
e)   To allow the prompt and effective investigation of the offence or of the conduct of the person in question.
f)   To prevent any prosecution for the offence from being hindered by the disappearance of the person in question.

Detention and interrogation

Detention

s.30 – The suspect must be taken to the police station as soon as possible after arrest unless required elsewhere.

s.36 – On arrival at the police station, the **custody officer** decides whether there is enough evidence to charge the suspect.

s.37 – If there is not yet sufficient evidence to charge, they will assess whether such evidence might be obtained through questioning and if so, a suspect may be detained for these purposes. If not then the suspect should be released. If enough evidence already exists to charge on arrest, the suspect should be granted bail under **s.38 PACE**.

s.40 – A person detained but not yet charged should have his detention reviewed after first 6 hours and then every 9 hours by the custody officer.

s.41 – Police can authorise detention without charge for up to 24 hours. This was increased to 36 hours **(s.42)** following the **Criminal Justice Act 2003**.

s.44 – Maximum period of detention is 96 hours on approval from Magistrates.

s.54 – Police may search an **arrested** person on arrival at the police station and seize any item they believe the suspect might use to cause physical injury to himself or any other person, damage property, to interfere with evidence, or to assist him to escape; or any item the constable has reasonable grounds for believing may be evidence relating to an offence.

Intimate searches and samples

s.55 – **Intimate search** – The police, on the authorisation of an inspector or above, have the power to carry out an intimate search of the body's orifices where the superintendent has reasonable grounds for believing that the suspect has concealed anything which he could use to cause physical injury to himself or others, and, he might use while he is in police detention or in the custody of a court; or that such a person may have a Class A drug concealed on him. The search must be carried out by a registered medical professional or a registered nurse.

s.62 – Intimate samples such as blood, saliva and semen can be taken from the suspect.

s.63 – Non-intimate samples such as hair and nail clippings can be taken if authorised by an inspector or above.

s.64 – DNA information can be extracted from the samples taken and placed indefinitely on national DNA database.

In the case of **S and Marper v UK (2008)** the ECHR ruled that it was a breach of Article 8 to retain DNA indefinitely if there was no conviction. Only DNA from individuals convicted of imprisonable offences can be stored indefinitely on the database.

s.61 and **s.27** Police can take fingerprints from suspects.

s.61A *PACE* as amended by **SOCPA (2005)** Impressions of footwear can be taken.

stretch&challenge

Sections 23-25 of the **Terrorism Act 2006** gave the circumstances when terror suspects could be detained for a 28-day period. This 'exceptional power' should have only been in force for 1 year and then reverted back to 14 days; however, it was renewed year on year with criticism from civil rights groups until January 2011 when it was not renewed and allowed to lapse back to 14 days. The **Protection of Freedoms** bill currently having gone through its second reading in Parliament seems to confirm that the detention period for terror suspects will be 14 days with no possibility of extension to 28 days.

stretch&challenge

A search of the mouth used to be classed as an intimate search. Drug dealers would frequently hide drugs in their mouths in the knowledge that the police could not search them. This gave them time to dispose of the evidence. **s.65 PACE** as amended by the **CJPOA 1994** now provides that a search of the mouth is a non-intimate search.

Art 8 ECHR - the right to respect for a persons private and family life, his home and his correspondence.

Key terminology

Admissible evidence can be used in court against the accused. When it comes to police powers, evidence must be properly obtained for it to be admissible.

Appropriate adult = parent, guardian or social worker.

Inadmissible = evidence that cannot be used in court against the accused.

Oppression = according to s.76(8) oppression means any torture, inhuman or degrading treatment or the use or threat of violence.

Synoptic link

Don't forget the right to consult a duty solicitor if a question asks you about the legal aid available for suspects. This is a popular synoptic question at A2 level.

Key case

R v Samuel (1988) – Suspect detained and questioned for armed robbery but refused access to solicitor on several occasions as police felt there was a danger other suspects could be warned. Samuel confessed to the offence. It was held that this was unjustified and the confessions could not be used in court.

R v Grant (2005) – Interference by the police in a person's right to consult with a solicitor was held to be so serious that his conviction for murder was quashed.

Rights and treatment of suspects during detention and interrogation

s.60 – Interviews should be tape recorded. However, it has been found that interviews can take place outside of the police station, for example on the way to the station. In some areas the police also video record interviews. The police must make a record of the interview and keep it on file.

s.56 – The suspect has the right to have someone informed of his arrest. This right can be suspended for up to 36 hours if it is felt that the person chosen by the suspect may interfere with the investigation in some way (e.g., alerting other suspects, destroying evidence, etc).

s.58 – The suspect has the right to consult a solicitor privately and free of charge. Again, this right can be suspended for up to 36 hours for the reasons mentioned above. This advice can be given over the telephone by **Criminal Defence Service Direct.**

s.57 – Vulnerable suspects, i.e. those under 17 and mentally disordered/disabled, must have an **appropriate adult** with them during questioning. This right is in addition to the s.58 right above. The absence of this person may render any confession **inadmissible** in court.

Code C – The suspect must be cautioned on arrest and before each interview.

Evidence and admissibility

It is essential that police powers are exercised correctly in order for the evidence obtained to be used in court (i.e. be admissible). The courts can refuse to admit evidence that has not been properly obtained.

s.76(2)(a) Confession evidence may be excluded at trial if obtained by **oppression**. If this is raised, it is then up to the prosecution to prove beyond reasonable doubt that the confession was *not* obtained by oppression.

s.76(2)(b) Confession evidence may be excluded at trial if it was obtained in circumstances which make it unreliable. See the cases of **Samuel** and **Grant** above where failure to provide access to legal advice rendered the confessions inadmissible.

s.78 Any evidence including a confession may be excluded under this section on the grounds that it would adversely affect the fairness of the trial. This includes situations such as not writing up the interviews straight after they had finished as in the case of **R v Canale (1990)**.

Breach of the Codes of Practice must be 'serious and substantial' in order for the evidence obtained to be considered for exclusion.

As stated above, under **s.57** vulnerable suspects, i.e. those under 17 and mentally disordered/disabled, must have an appropriate adult with them during questioning. The absence of this person may render any confession **inadmissible** in court. Under **s.77** the jury would be warned where a confession is made by a mentally-handicapped person.

The police have wide ranging powers that can be exercised with discretion. There is always the risk of misinterpretation of a situation and errors but the powers are essential in order to keep the public safe. Where there have been errors, remedies may be available.

When answering a question on this topic, be sure to include as many sections as you can and apply them to the facts of an LA3-style scenario. Remember to **define the law, apply the law** and **reach a conclusion on that point of law** before moving on to the next. Even if the police appear to have exercised their powers correctly, it is still important to discuss this in the same way rather than just concluding that it was correctly done. This is a very popular topic at A level.

Complaints against the Police

According to the Rule of Law, no one is above the law and everyone is equal under it. This also applies to the police. Even though the police have the power to lawfully infringe a person's human rights, such as the right to liberty under article 5, they must do so within the powers they have been given and without breaking any law. They should also adhere to the PACE Codes of Practice.

Anyone can make a police complaint. The complainant does not need to be a 'victim' of police misconduct. They might, for example, have been a witness to an incident, which they feel should be the subject of a complaint. The complaint should be made within one year and must be against a particular officer, group of officers or civilian staff. It is therefore important to get as many details about the officer(s) in question in order to file the complaint. General complaints about police policy/practice or local police may be made to the Home Office via the local MP or the local Police Authority.

In order to ensure the police act within the law, an aggrieved citizen can either make a complaint or sue through the civil courts. The police complaints procedure used to be overseen by the Police Complaints Authority (PCA) but due to wide criticisms, this was abolished by the *Police Reform Act 2002* which replaced the PCA with the **Independent Police Complaints Commission (IPCC)**. Their role is to investigate, supervise or manage complaints against the police and make sure they are dealt with effectively. It is hoped that this new body will be more independent, open and accessible than the PCA and that individuals feel more willing to make a complaint. An alternative or additional option is for the aggrieved person to take a civil action and sue the police.

This topic is going to explore the procedure for making a complaint, the role of the Independent Police Complaints Commission and the possibility of taking a civil action against the police.

Complaints procedure

All complaints start with the individual in question, or solicitor or MP on their behalf, making a written complaint to the police force in question. The Independent Police Complaints Commission does not have the power to record complaints and if a complaint is made to them, they must forward it to the relevant police force in question. In the majority of cases, complaints are considered and recorded by the Professional Standards Department (PSD) of the police force concerned. The PSD makes a decision on whether to record the complaint and if they choose not to record the complaint, the complainant has the right of appeal against this. The PSD then proceeds to decide if the complaint should be dealt with informally (under the 'local' or 'informal' resolution procedure). The likely outcome of a local resolution is an apology and there is no right of appeal once the local resolution is chosen. If the PSD decide the complaint is suitable for formal resolution then it will be dealt with through the local investigation procedure. This will require the police to appoint an Investigating Officer of the same rank or above as the officer being investigated. This Investigating Officer can be from the same force or a different one. The police have discretion to refer a matter to the IPCC and the IPCC can also decide to deal with any particular case if they choose.

stretch&challenge

The Rule of law is one of three key principles underpinning the UK constitution. AV Dicey's Rule of Law states that:

1. There should be no sanction without breach.
2. Everyone is equal before the law.
3. Rights of individuals are secured by decisions of judges in courts of law and not by a written constitution.

Grade boost

This topic is no longer examined as an essay-style question on LA4 Section A. It now comes up on LA3 as a problem scenario similar to the Police Powers question. You are likely to be faced with a scenario where a person's rights have been breached and asked to consider what the powers of the Independent Police Complaints Commission are to investigate the incident.

stretch&challenge

In the Metropolitan Police the Professional Standards Department is referred to as the Directorate of Professional Standards.

stretch&challenge

In the most serious cases, the IPCC will carry out a completely independent investigation. For slightly less serious cases the IPCC will manage a Police investigation ('managed' investigations). In the majority of cases the Police will deal with the complaint and the IPCC will supervise the investigation ('supervised' investigation) or the Police alone will deal with the case ('local investigation' not to be confused with 'local resolution').

Synoptic link

The CPS could come up as the synoptic link with an LA3 Police complaints question. A question may ask about the tests the CPS use to determine if they should go ahead with a prosecution against the Police officer. You would be expected to discuss the Full Code test and/or Threshold test in your answer.

stretch&challenge

Look up the incidents mentioned above and compile a report on what happened and what the conclusions of the IPCC investigations were.

Grade boost

Visit www.ipcc.gov.uk and explore the operation of the IPCC. Consider whether it is open, timely, proportionate and fair.

There are, however, occasions where a complaint must be forwarded to the IPCC. The IPCC may decide to investigate, supervise or manage the complaint. The local police must refer the following incidents to the IPCC and the IPCC can investigate these issues even if a complaint has not been made:

- Deaths following police contact (e.g. custody incident) or cases involving serious injury to a member of the public.
- Fatal road accidents involving a police vehicle.
- Use of a firearm by an officer on duty.
- Allegations of aggravated discriminatory behaviour.
- Allegations of assault.
- Allegations of 'hate' crime.
- Allegations that an officer has committed a serious arrestable offence while on duty.
- Allegations of corruption.

The IPCC can also refer a case to the Crown Prosecution Service if it believes that an officer should be prosecuted and this will be dealt with in the same way as a prosecution against a citizen.

The Independent Police Complaints Commission

The IPCC was established by the **Police Reform Act** and became operational in April 2004. According to its website – www.ipcc.gov.uk – its primary statutory purpose is to 'increase public confidence in the police complaints system in England and Wales'.

The IPCC was set up to replace the Police Complaints Authority, as the government felt a more independent, accessible and open service was needed to encourage individuals to come forward with complaints against the police and have confidence in the investigation. As discussed above, there are certain cases that they will independently investigate thereby taking control of the investigation from the police, but for the majority of cases the police are likely to be involved in some capacity. As well as the police force, the IPCC deals with complaints regarding HM Revenue and Customs, the Serious Organised Crime Agency (SOCA) and the UK Border Agency.

The IPCC is overseen by a Chair and 12 Commissioners. In order to promote fairness, by law none of the Commissioners or the Chair must have worked for the police in any capacity. The Commissioners are appointed by the Home Secretary.

Since its inception, the IPCC has been involved in some high profile investigations. The shooting on the London Underground of Jean Charles de Menezes, who was mistakenly believed to be a suicide bomber, is one of the most contentious cases they have had to deal with. The police were found to be in breach of health and safety rules and given a substantial fine. No criminal prosecution was taken. Since then they have had some further prominent cases to handle such as the death of Ian Tomlinson at the G20 protests and the shooting of Raoul Moat. It is likely that the IPCC will be involved in the investigations into the alleged phone hacking by the News of the World and the allegations that some police officers were paid to supply information.

Civil actions against the police

An individual may bring a civil action against the police and seek damages to compensate them for the injuries and loss sustained. When the PCA was in office, if a complainant's grievance against the police failed, this was not necessarily a bar to a successful civil action. Under the IPCC and its extended powers of investigation, it is yet to be seen whether the failure of a complaint will hinder the success of any civil action. The police can be sued under various categories such as: malicious prosecution, false imprisonment, wrongful arrest, trespass, assault or negligence. It is normal practice to sue the Chief Constable of the police force in question; therefore, unlike complaints, the individual identities of the officers need not be known. Cases are usually heard in the High Court and the decision and award of damages will be decided by a jury.

There have been a number of cases over the years where the police have been sued successfully. The case of **Goswell v Commissioner of Police for The Metropolis (1998)** is an example of a successful claim against the police. Mr Goswell was waiting in his car for his girlfriend when he was approached by PC Trigg who asked him to get out of his car without making any check upon the car. Mr Goswell began shouting and swearing and complaining that the police were unfairly troubling him and instead should have been out properly investigating a recent arson attack on his home. PC Trigg twice told Mr Goswell to calm down but he failed to do so. Mr Goswell was then taken hold of by the officers and handcuffed behind his back. PC Trigg struck Mr Goswell over the forehead with a police truncheon causing a wound which bled profusely. Mr Goswell was then put into a police car and taken to Woolwich police station. Only on arrival was he told why he had been arrested. He sued the police in the civil courts for assault and false imprisonment, and was awarded the considerable damages of £120,000 for assault, £12,000 for false imprisonment and £170,000 exemplary damages for arbitrary and oppressive behaviour. On appeal this was reduced to £47,600.

In the case of **The Commissioner of Police for the Metropolis v Thompson and Hsu (1997)** the Court of Appeal laid down important guidelines on the award of damages in civil cases against the police. Kenneth Hsu was originally awarded £220,000 in damages for wrongful arrest, false imprisonment and assault by the police but this was reduced on joint appeal (Thompson) to £35,000. Following these cases, the compensation awards have been limited due to concerns that the large awards given by juries diminished the budget available for policing. There is a current ceiling of £50,000 for exemplary damages for 'oppressive, arbitrary or unconstitutional behaviour' by the police.

Remedies for breach of police powers

It is important that there are adequate remedies in place to deter future similar behaviour and to provide the complainant with some form of resolution. Among the outcomes of both local resolution and other types of investigation are:

- An apology by the police force
- An explanation
- A change in policy or procedure
- A referral to the Crown Prosecution Service
- A recommendation that disciplinary action be taken
- Judicial review.

stretch&challenge

In a civil case, the standard of proof is 'on the balance of probabilities' and the burden lies with the claimant.

stretch&challenge

Judicial review – Takes place in the High Court and oversees the decisions of public bodies such as the Police. An application must be made by an individual who feels their rights have been infringed. If they breach their powers it may also result in a breach of an individual's rights and therefore the right to review the exercise of powers granted is an important remedy. In recent years, protestors who took part in the G20 demonstrations and complained that they were beaten and unlawfully restrained by the Police won a judicial review of the tactics used by the officers during the event. John Prescott has also won a judicial review into the Police inquiry into the phone hacking scandal.

Grade boost

These topics can be encountered on both papers – on LA3 as a synoptic question and on LA4 as an essay question.

>> Pointer

Typical questions on these topics for **LA4** may be:

CPS – Consider whether the Crown Prosecution Service has changed the criminal justice system in England and Wales for the better.

Bail – Evaluate the extent to which the law relating to bail maintains a fair balance between the rights of unconvicted defendants and the rights of the general public to be protected against crime.

These will be essay questions and will therefore be worth 25 marks.

It is important for these questions that you cover all three Assessment Objectives, that is, show Knowledge and Understanding, Skills and Communication. To do this, you need to explain everything you know about the CPS or Bail and then **evaluate** the CPS or Bail systems with reference to relevant legal authority.

>> Pointer

Typical questions on these topics for **LA3** may be:

CPS – Explain the tests used by the police to decide whether or not to prosecute.

Bail – Explain the powers of the police to grant bail.

Remember these will be part b) synoptic questions and will therefore be worth 11 marks, which test Knowledge and Understanding, so make sure you provide a thorough and detailed explanation and description of whatever the question is asking.

K AS and A2 Material overlap

There are some topics that you would have studied at AS that you need to know in detail for A2. All of these topics are contained in the AS Study and Revision Guide. These topics are:

- Crown Prosecution Service
- Bail
- Criminal Process and Appeals

CPS

You need to know:

- History and role of the Crown *Prosecution Service Prosecution of Offences Act 1985*
- Code for Crown Prosecutors **The Full Code Test, The Threshold Test**
- Role of the Attorney General
- Reforms of the Crown Prosecution Service

Narey (1998)	**Glidewell (1999)**
MacPherson (1999)	**Auld (2001)**
Abu Hamza (2006)	

The Public Prosecution Service: Setting the Standard (2009)

Bail

You need to know:

- Police bail – *s.38 Police and Criminal Evidence Act 1984, s.4 Criminal Justice Act 2003*
- Court bail – *s.4 Bail Act 1976*
- Conditional bail – *Criminal Justice and Public Order Act 1994*
- Restrictions on bail – *ss.14, 18, 19 Criminal Justice Act 2003*, *s.56 Crime and Disorder Act 1998*, *s.24 Anti-Terrorism*, *Crime and Security Act 2001*
- Advantages and disadvantages of bail

Criminal Trial Process and Appeals

You need to know:

- Classification of offences
- Procedure for triable either way offences
- Appeals from Magistrates' Court
- Youth offenders **Procedure Appeals**
- Procedure for summary offences
- Procedure for indictable offences
- Appeals from Crown Court

Role of the Attorney General

The Attorney General is a senior lawyer and has multi-faceted roles in both law and politics. The current Attorney General is **Dominic Grieve** and he was appointed by the coalition government in May 2010. Since the ***Constitutional Reform Act 2005***, and the abolition of the judicial element of the Lord Chancellor, the Attorney General is the only member of the government who is required to be legally qualified.

The Attorney General has four main roles:

Political: Government Minister

Legal: Chief Legal Adviser to the government

Superintendent of the prosecution services

Guardian of the 'public interest'.

In terms of the legal role of the Attorney General, he is **Superintendent of the Prosecution Services** and this involves a number of responsibilities:

- His consent is needed to prosecute certain categories of offence, including Official Secrets, corruption, explosives, incitement to racial hatred and certain terrorism offences.

- He has the power to refer *'unduly lenient'* sentences to the Court of Appeal.

- He has the power to refer points of law in criminal cases to the Court of Appeal.

- He has statutory responsibility, under the ***Prosecution of Offences Act 1985*** for the main prosecuting authorities, including the Crown Prosecution Service, the Serious Fraud Office and the Revenue and Customs Prosecution Office.

- He does not get involved in the day-to-day running of the Crown Prosecution Service, but he will be asked for advice in cases which are deemed to be high profile, sensitive or difficult.

The Attorney General is also **guardian of the 'public interest'**; this means that he has to ensure that the public interest is taken into account when deciding whether or not to bring or discontinue prosecutions in line with the **Full Code test**.

Sir Hartley Shawcross was Attorney General in 1951 and he famously said: *'It has never been the rule in this country – I hope it never will be – that suspected criminal offences must automatically be the subject of prosecution.'*

Youth offenders

The emphasis with youth offenders, which are those aged between 10 and 17, is to use out of court disposals wherever possible, but where court is necessary they are usually tried in the **Youth Court**. The Youth Court is a branch of the Magistrates' Court, and will often appear in the same building.

The Youth Court is chaired by specially trained Magistrates who will be adept in the necessary skills of sensitivity and understanding to deal with young offenders. The sentencing powers available in the Youth Court are both custodial and non-custodial; the maximum custodial sentence is a 24-month **Detention and Training Order**, and there is a plethora of community sentences at their disposal if custody is deemed unnecessary.

There are certain characteristics of the Youth Court that make the procedure very different to an adult court; namely:

- **Less formal**; court officials will not wear wigs or gowns in order to reduce the distress caused to the youth.
- **Private**; there is no press permitted nor is there a public gallery.
- The victim of the crime is not forced to attend; indeed it is expected that they do not.

When the youth has been arrested, it is decided by the police whether the youth will be remanded in custody or released on bail. After this, the procedure is reminiscent of that of a triable either way offence for an adult offender.

PLEAD GUILTY		PLEAD NOT GUILTY
	If the Magistrates do not feel their sentencing powers are sufficient, or if it is a very serious case, they have the power to refer the case to the Crown Court	
SENTENCING At Youth Court		**TRIAL** At Youth Court

Exam Practice and Technique

Exam Advice and Guidance

How exam questions are set

WJEC A2 Law aims to encourage students to:

- develop and sustain their enjoyment of, and interest in, law;
- develop knowledge and understanding of selected areas of law and the legal system in England and Wales;
- develop an understanding of legal method and reasoning;
- develop the techniques of logical thinking, and the skills necessary to analyse and solve problems by applying legal rules;
- develop the ability to communicate legal arguments and conclusions with reference to appropriate legal authority;
- develop a critical awareness of the changing nature of law in society;
- gain a sound basis for further study;
- develop knowledge of the rights and responsibilities of individuals as citizens including, where appropriate, an understanding of moral, spiritual and cultural issues;
- develop, where appropriate, skills in communication, application of number and information technology;
- improve, where appropriate, their own learning and performance, to facilitate work with others and solve problems in the context of their study of law.

Examination questions are written well in advance of the examination. They are written by the Principal examiner responsible for the unit. A committee of experienced examiners discuss the quality of every question and changes are made to the questions until the committee agree that they are appropriate. The questions are written to reflect the substantive content and the success criteria outlined in the specification.

Each of the papers LA3 and LA4 are weighted differently. LA3 is worth 20% of the A-Level and LA4 is worth 30% of the A-Level, making 50% of the total qualification; the other 50% coming from the AS examinations.

Exam answers are marked in relation to three assessment objectives:

- **Assessment Objective 1 (AO1) – Knowledge and Understanding**
  This is Knowledge and Understanding and it accounts for 18% of the marks at A2; divided between LA3 and LA4; 7.2% and 10.8% respectively.

  This assessment objective (AO) is assessing candidates' underlying knowledge and understanding of the workings of the law as described in the subject content. It is also assessing candidates' ability to describe how the law operates and applies in practice. To achieve the higher mark boundaries, candidates would be expected to bring in current debates, criticisms and major proposals for the law if applicable. Candidates are expected to bring in legal authority to support their answers as appropriate and required by the specification.

- **Assessment Objective 2 (AO2) – Skills**
  This is analysis and evaluation and accounts for 26% of the marks at A2; divided between LA3 and LA4; 10.4% and 15.6% respectively.

  This assessment objective is assessing candidates' ability to evaluate how the law operates and is implemented, and the extent to which it protects rights and imposes duties. It looks at how well candidates can categorise factual problems in order to apply relevant legal principles and conduct legal argument, applying law to facts and supporting conclusions by the citation of authority and by analysis and analogy. In this AO, candidates are expected to analyse and evaluate, interpret and use legal material including statutes and other sources of law.

- **Assessment Objective 3 (AO3) – Language and Argument**
  This accounts for 6% of marks at A2; divided between LA3 and LA4; 2.4% and 3.6% respectively.

  Use of key terminology and development of an argument is important in law. This assessment objective is looking at candidates' ability to present a logical and coherent argument and communicate relevant material in a clear and effective manner using appropriate legal terminology. It considers the extent to which candidates refer to specialist terms and conventions appropriate to the question and how they organise and present information, ideas, descriptions and arguments. It is also assessing candidates' ability to clearly express ideas and present their answers with accuracy in spelling, punctuation and grammar.

The A2 Law exam comprises two papers sat on separate days:

LA3

This paper is 1½ hours long and consists of four problem scenarios. Each question is broken down into part a) and b) totalling 25 marks. Part a) will assess your ability to apply the law to a given scenario and is worth a maximum of 14 marks and part b) will assess synoptic knowledge; that is, a topic that was covered as part of the AS specification and will be worth a maximum of 11 marks. Candidates have to answer two full questions from a choice of four (Part a) and b) of two questions). The paper is out of 50 marks in total.

LA4

This paper is 2½ hours long and consists of two sections. A total of three questions has to be answered across the paper.

SECTION A: This section consists of four essay question, of which the candidate has to choose two essays. Each essay is worth 25 marks. This is an opportunity for candidates to show the examiner everything they know about a topic; and it is important to show a range of knowledge, including recent criticisms and reforms as well as citing ample legal authority.

SECTION B: This section consists of two stimulus response questions, of which the candidate has to choose one question. Each question is broken down into part a) and part b) totalling 25 marks. Part a) will assess your ability to respond to the stimulus and draw on your own knowledge and is worth 11 marks. Part b) will assess synoptic knowledge, and will be worth 14 marks.

How Exam questions are marked

Questions are split into parts a) and b). Students are assessed on three 'assessment objectives' as summarised above and below.

Part a)

For part a) questions which are worth 14 marks, candidates can achieve a maximum of 13 marks for AO2 for a 'sound' answer. WJEC marking guidelines for law dictate that examiners can award either the top or bottom of a mark boundary (for example, if an answer is 'adequate', it can achieve either 7 marks or 10). This can seem strange but it allows for a good spread of marks and if a candidates answer is 'safely' within a mark boundary, it generally achieves the top of the boundary and if an answer is 'just' within a boundary, it achieves the bottom of the mark boundary. One of the three marks available for AO3 is awarded for part a). This is generally always awarded unless a candidate has not answered the question or spelling and punctuation are exceptionally poor.

Marks are allocated as below:

MARKS	AO3
1	Presents effective communication using appropriate legal terminology. Nonetheless, there may be several errors in grammar, punctuation and spelling, although not enough to detract from communication of meaning.
0	Fails to communicate and present logical argument, including inadequate use of legal terminology. There are significant errors of grammar, punctuation and spelling which detract from communication of meaning.

MARKS	AO2 Skills
11–13	Candidates demonstrate a sound evaluation of how the law operates, or an accurate and well-substantiated application of the law to a given fact situation. This is achieved through their selection of legal authorities, by appropriate methodologies and by their ability to apply the law to a given question. They support their conclusions by citation, analysis and analogy.
7–10	Candidates demonstrate an adequate evaluation of how the law operates, or a generally accurate and substantiated application of the law to a given fact situation. This is achieved through their selection of legal authorities, by appropriate methodologies and by their ability to apply the law to a given question and support their conclusions by citation.
3–6	Candidates demonstrate a limited evaluation of some of the points of how the law operates, or apply the law to a given fact situation in a partly accurate and occasionally unsubstantiated way. This is achieved through a limited selection of legal authorities and limited ability to apply the law to a given question.
0–2	Candidates demonstrate a basic evaluation of one of the simpler points of how the law operates or apply the law to a given factual situation in a generally inaccurate and unsubstantiated way. There will be little or no reference to legal authorities and points will not be developed. There will be very limited evidence of structure in the candidate's response.

Part b

For part b) questions which are worth 11 marks, candidates can achieve a maximum of nine marks for AO1 for a 'sound' answer. Two of the three marks available for AO3 are awarded for part b). Here the two marks are awarded based on the general overall quality of a candidates answer and assessed according to the definition of AO3 below.

Marks are allocated as below:

MARKS	AO3
2	Presents a wholly logical and coherent argument and provides clear application using appropriate legal terminology. This does not mean that there are no errors in grammar, punctuation and spelling but these will only be occasional.
1	Presents a mostly logical and coherent argument and provides a reasonably adequate application using appropriate legal terminology. Whilst there may be errors in grammar, punctuation and spelling, these are not enough to detract from a mostly effective communication of meaning.

MARKS	AO1 Knowledge and Understanding
8–9	Candidates display a sound knowledge and understanding of the subject content relevant to the question and a good perception of the concepts and principles underlying that subject content.
6–7	Candidates display an adequate knowledge and understanding of the subject content relevant to the question and have a perception of some of the concepts and principles underlying that subject content. They display a general understanding of the practical application of the law and are aware of aspects of current debate and criticism.
3–5	Candidates display a limited knowledge and understanding of the subject content relevant to the question with limited insight into some of the concepts and principles underlying that subject content. They display a limited understanding of the practical application of the law and are aware in general terms of some of the current criticisms.
0–2	Candidates display a basic knowledge and understanding of the subject content relevant to the question and/or indentify some of the relevant principles. They demonstrate occasional basic insights into some of the concepts and principles underlying the subject content. They display a basic understanding of the practical application of the law.

LA4

SECTION A: For these questions, the full range of marks is available for all three assessment objectives; that is 13 for AO1, 9 for AO2 and 3 for AO3. Therefore, in order to achieve full marks, candidates need to demonstrate a sound knowledge, as well as an awareness of legal authority and ability to provide critique and reference to current issues surrounding the area.

SECTION B: These questions are split into part a) and part b), which are worth 11 and 14 marks respectively.

Part a) assesses AO1 Knowledge and Understanding, with a maximum of 11 marks, as shown above. Part b) assesses AO2 Skills, with a maximum of 14 marks, as shown above.

Improving your exam performance

There are a few important things to remember and common errors that occur year on year:

- Where the question has a part a) and a part b), you MUST answer part a) and b) from the SAME question. Many candidates year after year pick and choose, but these rubric errors will get you no marks.

- It is good practice to write a good introduction to your answer because it shows the examiner that you understand the topic from the start. Do not fall into the trap of writing a 'waffly' introduction; spend a couple of minutes thinking and planning before you begin to write;

In an essay question, your introduction should begin with a definition of key terms contained in the question. Some examples are highlighted below:

'Evaluate the effectiveness of the Crown Prosecution Service when deciding whether or not to charge a suspect'

'Evaluate the extent to which intoxication by alcohol and other drugs can be used as a defence to a criminal charge'

In a problem question, you could revise a standard introduction for each topic. Here is an example of a Police Powers introduction:

Powers of the police to search, arrest and detain suspects are primarily governed by the Codes of Practice contained in the ***Police and Criminal Evidence Act 1984*** and amendments made by the ***Serious Organised Crime and Police Act 2005***. This legislation was enacted to uphold the defendant's ***Article 6 ECHR*** right to a fair trial and to provide accountability for the police to avoid the miscarriages of justice experienced in the 1970s by the likes of the ***Birmingham Six***, ***Guildford Four*** and ***Judith Ward***, whilst still allowing the police to carry out their primary function which is to maintain law and order and keep the public safe. Breach of this legislation could result in evidence becoming inadmissible in court and the defendant receiving a remedy through the civil courts. This scenario concerns the actions of the police, and I shall consider, in turn, whether their actions were lawful.

- Use as much legal authority as you can remember – this is especially important when you are applying the law in LA3, or making a critique in LA4. You also need to make sure you explain the relevance of the legal authority.

Example: Osman v DPP (1999)

Answer A: *Under **s.2 Police and Criminal Evidence Act 1984**, the police must give the suspect their name and station, as well as the object of the search; this was seen in the case of **Osman v DPP (1999)***

Answer B: *Under **s.2 Police and Criminal Evidence Act 1984**, the police must give the suspect their name and station, as well as the object of the search; this was seen in the case of **Osman v DPP (1999)**, where the defendant had his conviction quashed because the police failed to comply with s.2.*

The highlighted section of Answer B shows that the candidate knows and understands the relevance of the case, whereas the candidate in Answer A has just used the case to support her point and not actually made the progression in showing HOW.

- When answering part a) of an LA3 question, it is crucial that you STATE THE LAW and then APPLY THE LAW to the scenario. Let us consider the problem question on p79, and plan the answer. Remember it is critically important to cite sections from the relevant legislation. Examiners comment that there is a reluctance for candidates to cite sections of PACE, even though there may be an implication that the candidate does know what section applies. This is just a snippet of the problem question to show how an answer may be planned.

STATE LAW	APPLY LAW
Under **s.36 Police and Criminal Evidence Act 1984**, the suspect must be taken to the police station as soon as possible and a custody record must be opened.	There was nobody available to act as custody officer, as it must be someone of sergeant rank or above, and so therefore the police officer in Oscar's case acted unlawfully.
Under **s.56 Police and Criminal Evidence Act 1984**, the suspect has the right to have someone informed of his arrest. This right can be suspended for up to 36 hours if it is felt that the person chosen by the suspect may interfere with the investigation in some way by alerting other suspects or destroying evidence.	Oscar requested to telephone his wife, but this was denied and is clearly a breach of PACE.
Under **s.58 Police and Criminal Evidence Act 1984**, the suspect has the right to consult a solicitor privately and free of charge. Again, this right can be suspended for up to 36 hours for the reasons mentioned above. This advice can be given over the telephone by Criminal Defence Service Direct.	Oscar was denied the right to legal advice because the police officer did not have the time to contact him. This was clearly a breach of PACE, as there is nothing in the scenario to indicate that Oscar may interfere with the investigation. This was highlighted by the case of **R v Samuel (1988)** where confessions obtained after continued refusals to legal advice were held to be inadmissible in court.
Under **s.40 Police and Criminal Evidence Act 1984**, a person detained but not yet charged should have his detention reviewed after first 6 hours and then every 9 hours by the custody officer. Under **s.41 Police and Criminal Evidence Act 1984**, the superintendent can authorise detention without charge for up to 24 hours. This was increased to 36 hours (**s.42**) following the Criminal Justice Act 2003. **s.44 Police and Criminal Evidence Act 1984** allows for a maximum period of detention of 96 hours on approval from Magistrates.	Oscar was held for 37 hours, and there was no suggestion that his detention and well-being was reviewed; in fact the deprivation of food and water was a breach of his human rights and PACE. Oscar should have had his detention reviewed after 6 hours, and then every 9 hours. There is also no indication that approval was sought to detain him longer than 36 hours by the superintendent. It could be the case that because of this unlawful behaviour, any evidence gained during this time could be inadmissible in court.

- Part b) requires you to draw on synoptic knowledge from the AS course. It is always worth mentioning how the knowledge will apply to the scenario. For example, if part b) is on bail, you should consider whether the defendants you have mentioned in part a) would have been granted bail or not, and why. This is a useful conclusion to make, and will show the examiner that you can apply your knowledge to a given scenario.

- The synoptic links can be on anything from your AS course, and it is very difficult to predict what the link will be. The table below shows previous synoptic links, but remember this is just what has happened in the past, and is no indication of what may or may not come up in the future.

	Legal Funding	Crown Prosecution Service	Bail	Judge and/or Jury	Appeals
Homicide	✓ ✓				✓
Offences Against the Person		✓	✓		✓
Police Powers		✓	✓	✓	
Defences	✓			✓	
IPCC		✓			

- Remember to revise ALL the AS material, do not try to answer the question based on previous knowledge. You need to make sure you have as in-depth a knowledge as you did at AS and have an awareness of current reforms and criticisms in the area.

- Where possible, try to cite the legal authority in full. An attempt at citation will be credited, but obviously it is more appropriate to learn the cases and relevant legal authority.

Answer A: *Where the police refuse the suspect a solicitor, they are acting unlawfully, for example in one case the defendant had his conviction quashed because he had been unlawfully refused a solicitor.*

Answer B: *Where the police refuse the suspect a solicitor, they are acting unlawfully, for example in R v Samuel (1988), the defendant had his conviction quashed because he had been unlawfully refused a solicitor.*

It is quite clear that Answer A knows the case, but obviously the fact that the candidate in Answer B has actually cited it in full makes it more clear to the examiner that there is a sound knowledge, rather than just an adequate knowledge.

- Be aware of recent reforms, criticisms and current affairs in the area. Your lecturer may have made you aware of some such reports and news, but it is always good practice to keep abreast of recent developments. Bookmark these websites:

General websites – these are good for news articles and provide examples of recent developments that are of general public importance.

BBC – www.bbc.co.uk

The Guardian – www.guardian.co.uk

The Times – www.thetimes.co.uk

The Independent – www.independent.co.uk

The Daily Telegraph – www.telegraph.co.uk

Subject-specific websites – these are websites that will give you access to specific information on certain topics.

ACAS – www.acas.org.uk

Crown Prosecution Service – www.cps.gov.uk

Home Office – www.homeoffice.gov.uk

Parliament – www.parliament.uk

Ministry of Justice – www.justice.gov.uk

Directgov – www.direct.gov.uk

- Make sure you answer the question; many candidates will have learned essays off by heart, and then merely repeat this in the examination, only to find that it does not actually answer the question at all. Read and re-read the question to ensure that your planned answer actually answers the question.

- When you are revising, be careful if you are taking the decision to omit certain topics. It is very likely that a question may be asked which 'mixes' up topics, and you may find that you can answer part a but have not done enough revision to answer part b as competently. Look back over past papers and see what combination of topics have been asked.

- The stimulus response questions in LA4 are NOT comprehension exercises. You are required to use the stimulus as a source to support what you are saying, but ultimately, you are being examined on YOUR knowledge. Rewriting a table in your own words, or quoting copious amounts from the source is not going to get you any marks.

- You are marked on your use of appropriate legal terminology and your understanding of core legal principles; yet candidates often make very simple errors.

Do you know the difference between:

- *ECJ and ECHR?*
- *CPS and CPR?*
- *Guilty and Liable?*
- *Magistrates and Juries?*
- *'Should of' and 'Should have'?*

As obvious as these errors may seem, they are very common, so make sure you have a good grasp and watch your spelling:

- *Defendant*
- *Sentence*
- *Precedent*
- *Trial*

- Human Rights are an underpinning principle of most of the legal system now, and as such it is expected to be present across the examination in every topic. Therefore, it is important that you have a good grasp of the **Human Rights Act 1998**, as well as the key Articles of the **European Convention on Human Rights**.

Questions and Answers

1. LA3 Police Complaints

Study the text below and answer the questions based on it.

Harold borrowed a length of piping from his brother-in-law so that he could mend his central heating system. He put the piping in the bag and walked home. It was a warm evening and he was sweating. Part of the piping pointed out of the top of the bag. George, a member of the public, walked past Harold and thought that the piping looked like a shotgun. He telephoned the police and told them: 'I have just seen a nervous looking man with a shotgun.' As Harold approached his home, he was challenged by several members of a Police Armed Response Unit. Harold was surprised, and turned to face the direction where the challenge had come from. Susan, an armed police officer, immediately opened fire. Harold was killed immediately. Later that night the Chief Constable released a press statement incorrectly claiming that Harold had ignored the challenge from the officers of the Armed Response Unit and had threatened the police officers.

a) Consider the powers of the Independent Police Complaints Commission to investigate the incident. *(14 marks)*

Tom's answer: Grade D

① Clearly Susan has made a mistake and Harold's family should be entitled to make a complaint against her and possibly sue for a large sum of money. It is important that people are entitled to make complaints against the police and to do this they complain to the Independent Police Complaints Commission (IPCC).

② The IPCC replaced the Police Complaints Authority which was felt not to be independent enough for people to come forward with complaints. No police officer past or present can be a member of the IPCC which is good for the independence of the IPCC.

③ There are two types of complaint – formal and local resolution. Local or informal resolution is not suitable for this case as it is too serious and the mistake has led to someone dying. Formal resolution may mean that Susan is dismissed or disciplined. The police will then maybe refer the case to the IPCC so that they can run the investigation as it is not always appropriate for the police to investigate some serious complaints.

④ Or, Harold's family could sue the police. This is likely to result in lots of compensation for Harold's family as he died at the hands of the police. He was not armed and she shouldn't have shot back at him without checking fully that he was armed. Saying that, the police do a really important job and they do make mistakes.

Examiner commentary

① Tom has provided a brief introduction here and set out that the police can be sued and that people are entitled to make complaints against the police. He has also done well to give the name of the IPCC as the authority to which complaints are referred. He needs to be careful with his use of words here as he seems to say that complaints are made to the IPCC which is not correct. Complaints are made to the police who then refer the case to the IPCC.

② Tom gives a brief history of the replacement of the PCA with the IPCC and touches very briefly upon why. However, he doesn't cite the Police Reform Act 2002 as relevant legal authority here.

③ Good mention of both local and formal resolution here but there is a lack of explanation. He also again touches upon the remedies and the fact that serious cases are referred to the IPCC but he could do with mentioning the mandatory referral procedure. He also lacks depth in his explanations. Tom should also have considered the role of the CPS in determining whether an officer should be prosecuted.

④ Good progression on to the possibility of taking a civil action but Tom's answer again lacks depth. He could have discussed the fact a case is taken to the High Court, and given some key cases such as Goswell and also Kenneth Hsu as well as considering the limits placed on damages levels. He should also have given a conclusion in the final paragraph and summarised the main issues. As this is an LA3 problem scenario question, Tom should also have brought in the facts of the case a little more throughout including in the conclusion.

Mark awarded:
AO2 – 6
AO3 – 1
Total = 7 out of 14 (50% Grade D)

This is a limited answer from Tom. Though he touches upon several key issues such as formal and local resolution, as well as mentioning the IPCC which replaced the PCA, his answer generally lacks depth of explanation and legal authority to substantiate. There were only a few cases/ Acts relevant to this unit but because of this, they needed to be cited to achieve marks in the adequate or sound bands.

Seren's answer: Grade A

① The Police are accountable to their chief constable (the head of their police force) and the Local Police Authority who work with the chief constable to maintain an efficient and effective local police force. Both of these bodies are ultimately answerable to the Home Secretary who has overall control of the 43 police forces in England and Wales. When a complaint is made it was monitored by the Police Complaints Authority, which was replaced with the Independent Police Complaints Commission following the Police Reform Act 2002. Should it be found that a police officer or group of police officers have acted outside of their powers, the Director of Public Prosecutions is informed, who will then decide if the prosecution of the person in question should be allowed to continue. Any person who feels that the police have acted wrongly can make a written complaint either themselves or through a solicitor. There are advice bureaus and legal firms who specialise in pursuing and advising in complaints against the police.

② To make a complaint, the IPCC advises the following methods: contacting your local police force, attending a police station in person or contacting a solicitor or MP who can make a complaint on your behalf against the police. It is also possible to email, phone or fax the IPCC themselves. The IPCC themselves only investigate the most serious of complaints, with the vast majority being dealt with by the police force concerned. When submitting a written complaint, either by post or online, it is important to include the name of the police force involved, where and when the incident happened that led to your complaint, the circumstances that led to your complaint and your consent for the IPCC to pass the complaint onto the police force concerned. Details of who was involved, what was said/done, any damage or injury caused and details of any witnesses are also essential in making a complaint.

③ The IPCC can supervise, manage or investigate a complaint but a complaint can't be made directly to them, it has to go via the Professional Standards Department of the police station. A person should make a complaint in writing and include much information as I have said above. The PSD decide whether to record the complaint and if they do then a person's complaint will be dealt with either formally or informally. An informal complaint, which would be inappropriate here, would normally result in an apology. This case involving Harold and Susan would not go via informal resolution as Harold has been killed. His family could make a complaint but it would be passed to the IPCC due to the fact that someone has been shot and killed by the police. Cases like these are instantly passed to the IPCC. This is known as a mandatory referral.

④ In Harold's case there has been a clear case of mistaken identity and Susan opened fire far too quickly and without checking. This is similar to the case of Jean Charles de Menezes who was shot on the London Underground after mistaking him for a terrorist bomber. The local police must refer this incident to the IPCC and the IPCC can investigate these issues even if a complaint has not been made. As a death has occurred and an officer has used a firearm, this is such a case.

⑤ The IPCC can also refer the case to the CPS who will see if a prosecution should be brought against Susan for what seems to be an unlawful killing. This will be dealt with in the same way as a prosecution against a citizen.

⑥ Should Harold's family choose to also go with a Civil Action, in other words suing the police, it will be heard in the High Court. Such a case may result in compensation, which is now limited to £35,000 after the Kenneth Hsu case where he had his arms twisted, was put in a neck lock and bundled into a police van that resulted in bruising to his back. It was then decided by the court of appeal that a ceiling should be placed on cases against the police, as Kenneth Hsu was initially awarded £220,000, which was seen as outrageous and was not financially viable considering the high number of complaints that could potentially go to the High Court.

⑦ In conclusion, the IPCC would automatically investigate the case and they are independent, impartial and open. They have powers of investigation and will look at this case automatically as someone has died at the hands of the police. In addition, Harold's family could take a civil action against the police and Susan could be prosecuted by the CPS.

Examiner commentary

① A good opening paragraph putting the answer in context. Good citation of the Police Reform Act 2002 which established the IPCC, replacing the PCA. Though Seren has mentioned later on some of the reasons for the establishment of the IPCC, they would have been better placed here. Seren has also done well to discuss some of the ways that a complaint can be made.

② Seren has repeated some information in the beginning of this paragraph, but she does develop these points. She has given a good discussion of the importance of details in making a complaint, which is important for making a complaint.

③ Seren has now progressed on to the procedure for making a complaint. She has done well to bring in the Professional Standards Department and their role. She has also done well to discuss informal and formal resolution. As this is an LA3 question, some reference and application to the facts is key. Seren has correctly identified that this case is inappropriate for informal resolution as there has been a death following police contact and use of a firearm by an officer. She also does well to

cite the key term 'mandatory referral' for the fact that this case would be automatically referred to the IPCC even if a complaint is not made by the deceased's family.

④ Further development given in this paragraph and a good contemporary example given to support her answer. It is good practice to bring in contemporary examples and show an awareness of current affairs where possible. There are other recent examples that could have been cited here such as Ian Tomlinson and the G20 protests.

⑤ An important point made in this paragraph about the fact that the case may be referred to the CPS who will decide whether a prosecution should be taken against Susan.

⑥ Seren has logically progressed on to the possibility of civil actions against the police. She has done well to cite the case of Kenneth Hsu and discussed the limits placed on damages awarded in such cases also discussing the rationale behind this limit.

⑦ A good conclusion given though it would have been preferable to bring in the reasons for the establishment of the IPCC

earlier in the essay. Seren could also have considered the limits on the power of the IPCC as they cannot award compensation or discipline police officers. Apart from these minor points, this is a nice summary to conclude the essay.

Mark awarded:
AO2 – 12
AO3 – 2
Total = 14 out of 14 (100% Grade A)

This is a good answer with a sound range of issues discussed. Seren has worked logically through the procedure for making a complaint and accurately used a range of appropriate legal terminology. There is a limited amount of legal authority relevant to this question but the ones she has included are correct and well used to substantiate her answer. She has done more than just describe the procedure but has, importantly, applied this to the facts of the scenario which is essential for LA3 problem style questions. Seren has produced a logical and well-structured essay and accurately described and applied almost all the legal issues.

b) Describe the tests the Crown Prosecution Service will use when onsidering whether or not to prosecute Susan.

(11 marks)

Tom's answer: Grade D

① In this case there are a lot of witnesses who could give evidence against Susan the police officer. It is also wrong that she didn't check that Harold was armed. The CPS is there to decide whether a person should be prosecuted for a criminal offence. They were established under the PofO Act. They now also decide whether a person should be charged with an offence.

② To do this, they apply two tests – the evidential test and the public interest test. The evidential test looks at the evidence available and whether this can be used in court. If a case passes this test, it moves on to the public interest test where they look at whether a case is in the public interest to prosecute. They weigh up factors for and against the public interest such as whether a person is a racist and whether a person was really old committing the offence.

③ So, in this case, there is evidence against Susan as there are witnesses and she shot her gun at a person who was unarmed. A prosecution is likely against Susan.

Examiner commentary

① Tom jumps straight in to some of the facts of the scenario before putting his answer in context. This opening statement should be his introduction where he sets out the establishment of the CPS, their role and the Code for Crown Prosecutors. He also fails to give the full title of the Prosecution of Offences Act. He gives a brief mention of the decision to charge but doesn't expand on this and there is no mention of the threshold test.

② Tom does well to mention the two tests though should have first cited the Code for Crown Prosecutors. He could have brought in some facts of the scenario here to determine if there is sufficient evidence. He does well to mention that a case that doesn't pass the evidential test will not proceed no matter how important, but he then needed to consider a much wider range of public interest factors that he again could have applied to the facts of the scenario.

③ A very brief and unsubstantiated conclusion that is a far from satisfactory end to this answer. He attempts some application here but this would have been better placed elsewhere.

Mark awarded:
AO1 – 5
AO3 – 1
Total = 6 out of 11 (55% Grade D)

An upper 'limited' answer. Tom has touched upon several relevant areas but his answer lacks depth and specific explanation. It is a superficial answer touching upon some relevant areas but failing to adequately describe or evaluate them. He also fails to include some fundamental Acts such as the full title of the Prosecution of Offences Act 1985 and the Criminal Justice Act. He also needed to accurately discuss the Code for Crown Prosecutors, bring in a wider range of public interest factors and the threshold test. All in all, a brief and unsophisticated answer.

Seren's answer: Grade A

① The CPS has to follow two tests when deciding whether or not to prosecute a person. The same applies to a police officer as it would to a private citizen. The Prosecution of Offences Act 1985 established the CPS as a central prosecuting body. Section 10 of this Act contains the Code for Crown Prosecutors which is where the two tests are found. These are applied to determine whether a person should be prosecuted for an offence or not.

② The first test is the evidential test, which looks at whether there is sufficient evidence to prosecute a person. They look at how reliable the evidence is and whether there are credible witnesses and evidence. In this case, there seem to be several witnesses such as George and the other armed officers. There is also the evidence of the fact the police gun has been shot and that Harold was not himself carrying a gun.

③ If a case passes the evidential test, it progresses on to the public interest test. It is important to note that if a case doesn't pass the evidential test, it will not proceed on to the public interest test no matter how important. When they assess the public interest test, they apply factors for and against the public interest. They balance these factors. Some factors for the public interest are: use of a weapon, committing a crime against a person serving the public and a racially motivated crime. There are also factors against the public interest such as if the crime was committed by a very old or very young person or if the person is mentally disordered. None of these seem to apply in this case but it might seem to be in the public interest as a weapon was used. However, it was not the use of a weapon in the 'criminal' sense as the police officer Susan felt she was doing her job correctly. It is a difficult job and sometimes the police make mistakes. There is a factor against the public interest for genuine mistakes which may be the case here.

④ The CPS now also decides whether to go ahead with a charge against a person following the Criminal Justice Act 2003. For this they use the Threshold test. They will use this to decide whether to charge Susan.

Examiner commentary

① A good opening statement where Seren has cited the Prosecution of Offences Act 1985. She puts her answer in context by mentioning the two tests that are used and the Code for Crown Prosecutors. It is also good that she specifically stated s.10 as legal authority.

② Seren discusses the evidential test here and gives a good level of depth on the factors taken into account. She also does well to mention the scenario as this is an LA3 style question and requires some application to the facts. Good use of key legal terms here.

③ Logical progression here on to the public interest test. Seren has considered factors for and against the public interest, which is key for this test. She appeared to be concluding that there are no factors against the public interest, but then recognises, importantly, that there is a factor against for genuine mistake which may be a factor in this case.

④ Perhaps an afterthought but still good to see the Threshold test mentioned with citation of the CJA 2003. As a result, there is a lack of a conclusion to this answer from Seren, though she has done enough to get into the 'sound' category.

Mark awarded:
AO1 – 8
AO3 – 2
Total = 10 out of 11 (91% Grade A)

Seren has done well with this synoptic question. She has discussed the Code for Crown Prosecutors accurately and applies the two tests well to the facts using key terminology appropriately. She also works logically through the issues from the evidential test to the public interest test. Her answer lacks a clear introduction and conclusion but there is still a lot of detail and citation of the relevant Acts for Seren to achieve a mark in the 'sound' category.

2. LA3 Non-Fatal Offences

Q&A

Study the text below and answer the questions based on it.

Abdul lives on the third floor of a block of flats. He was cooking his evening meal when the frying pan caught fire. Abdul was unable to put out the flames, so in desperation he threw the blazing frying pan out of the window. The frying pan struck Deirdre, who was walking along the street with her husband, Ken. Deirdre suffered a fractured skull and severe burns to her face. Ken fainted from shock. Hearing Deidre's screams, Abdul rushed downstairs and performed first aid on them both while waiting for an ambulance to arrive. Ken regained consciousness while Deidre was being placed in the ambulance. Dazed and confused, he aimed a punch at Abdul, but missed and hit Steve, a paramedic, giving him a black eye.

a) In the light of reported case law and other sources of law, consider whether Abdul and Ken may have committed any offences, taking account of any defences which may be available to them. *(14 marks)*

Tom's answer: Grade D

① I have been asked to advise Abdul and Ken on their actions and consider their criminal liability and what defences are available.

② Abdul can be seen to be criminally liable for causing a fractured skull and severe burns to Deirdre. Under s.20 Offences against the Person Act 1861 he can be held criminally liable for malicious wounding and causing grievous bodily harm. The actus reus for s.20 is to cause GBH. I believe Abdul has fulfilled this as Deirdre has suffered a fractured skull and severe burns. A case to highlight this is DPP v Smith where they said it had to be really serious harm. This is really serious harm.

③ The mens rea for s.20 is shown by recklessness or by intention. It is shown that Abdul has fulfilled the mens rea as he was reckless in throwing the pan out of the window.

④ s.20 is an indictable offence which can carry a prison sentence of 5 years. I believe Abdul could use necessity as a defence as it was necessary to throw the pan out of the window to save harming himself. In the case of Re: A (children) this defence was used as the lesser of two evils. To show necessity as a defence it must be shown that the actions prevented a greater evil. Abdul's whole apartment could have caught fire and lots of people could have died. Throwing the pan out probably caused less damage.

⑤ Ken can be criminally liable for punching Steve as he caused him to have a black eye. This could be Actual Bodily Harm (ABH). The actus reus is causing actual bodily harm as in the case of Miller. The mens rea is intention or recklessness. Although Ken meant to strike Abdul but actually hit the paramedic Steve this doesn't matter.

⑥ There is also a defence of duress here that Abdul could try to claim as he needed to throw out the pan to stop himself being harmed. So, there are various offences and defences available.

Examiner commentary

① It is preferable not to use the first person in an academic answer. Students should ideally write in the third person.

② Tom has done well to identify GBH as a likely offence with which Abdul could be charged. He has cited the correct statute and section and also included the Smith case. There is a general lack of depth in his answer but a good effort. He should also make the point that plea bargaining could happen and so it is not certain which offence he would ultimately be charged with. With this in mind, all potential offences should be considered.

③ He has progressed on to the mens rea here which is a good approach though this is a little brief. It is not merely 'intention or recklessness' but has a wider definition. He should also be sure to include *subjective* recklessness. He has attempted to apply the law to the facts but again needs to do this with greater evaluation.

④ Good background information given on s.20 but s.20 is not an indictable offence; it is a triable either way offence. It is important to get this right. It is also good to see Tom discuss the defence of necessity which could apply here. He is generally correct with his definition and includes the relevant case of Re: A to substantiate.

⑤ Tom has now progressed on to Steve and his black eye. He has done well to deal with each incident separately as this is the preferable approach but he needs a lot more on the actus reus and mens rea of ABH including citing s.47 OAP Act 1861. He also hints at transferred malice in striking Ken but hitting Steve instead but needed to use the correct legal term here.

⑥ Tom mentions duress as a defence which is relevant but doesn't expand on this. This is a valid point that with a little more explanation and case law could have helped him achieve the top of the mark boundary.

Mark awarded:
AO2 – 7
AO3 – 1
Total = 8 out of 14 (57% Grade D)

This is an adequate answer at the lower end of the mark boundary. Though Tom has introduced a lot of relevant concepts, he doesn't adequately expand on them and there is a lack of legal terminology, authority and range at times in his answer. He needed to consider a wider range of offences such as battery and assault and needed to substantiate with a wider range case law to illustrate. He also needed to be more specific with his definitions of the actus reus and mens rea of each offence. With a few tweaks, Tom could easily have achieved the top of this mark boundary (10 marks) and increased his grade to a low B for this question.

Seren's answer: Grade A

① I have been asked to advise Abdul and Ken taking into consideration any defences available to them. I will begin by looking at Abdul. The law on non-fatal offences is contained in common law but also the Offences against the Person Act 1861 (OAP Act). Usually some unofficial plea bargaining can take place between offences so I will consider a range of offences with which each person could be charged.

② The first offence Abdul could be charged with is malicious wounding or inflicting grievous bodily harm under s.20 OAP Act 1861. This is a triable either way offence and carries a maximum sentence of 5 years imprisonment. The actus reus is infliction of GBH or a wound which is a breaking of the external skin according to the case of C (A Minor) v Eisenhower. It could be argued that Abdul has inflicted GBH on Deirdre by fracturing her skull and she may also have a wound through the burns. The case of Bollom says the injuries don't have to be life threatening though we are not told the extent of her injury here and in R v Brown and Stratton injuries such as bruising, broken nose, missing teeth and concussion were held to be grievous bodily harm. The mens rea is either intention or recklessness to inflict some harm according to the case of Mowatt and the case of DPP v A. If we apply this to the facts, I don't think Abdul has intention but he has probably been reckless as it is foreseeable that someone could be harmed if he throws a burning pan out of the window.

③ OAP Act s.18 would not apply here as s.18 requires intention to cause grievous bodily harm which Abdul doesn't have. They could plea bargain down to s.47 which is ABH. This is another triable either way offence and also carries a maximum sentence of 5 years. As we are not told much information about her injuries, it could be ABH but is more likely to be GBH. The actus reus of ABH is an assault or battery that causes actual bodily harm. There is a battery as the pan has hit Deirdre (unlawful application of force) and it has caused actual bodily harm which is defined in Miller as 'any hurt or injury calculated to interfere with health or comfort'. The case of Chan Fook says the injury doesn't have to be permanent but mustn't be so trivial as to be insignificant. The mens rea is the same as for assault or battery so is easier to prove (R v Savage and Parmenter). The mens rea for battery is intention or subjective recklessness to apply unlawful force. I think both the actus reus and mens rea could be proved here as Abdul was reckless in applying unlawful force – he should have realised that he would hit someone below by throwing a pan out of the window.

④ The fact that Abdul also caused Ken to faint could mean that he would be charged with either assault or battery. The actus reus for an assault is causing the victim to fear that force is about to be used against them immediately. In the case of Smith v CC Woking police it was held to be immediate even though the defendant was standing outside and her door was locked. The mens rea is intention or subjective recklessness to cause the victim to fear the application of unlawful force. Abdul doesn't mean to frighten anyone here so it is more likely to be a battery. The actus reus of battery can be indirectly applied as in the case of Haysted v DPP. He was also subjectively reckless as he should have realised someone could have been hit by the pan.

⑤ The punch that Ken gave the paramedic could be an ABH again as it gave him a black eye. It is a battery that caused ABH and he intended to do so even though he was dazed and confused. It is more than trivial as in the case of Chan Fook and would cause discomfort as in Miller. Here we also need to consider transferred malice as his punch was aimed at Ken, not the paramedic, Steve. As long as a person has malice towards one person it can be transferred to the person that they actually hit as in the case of Latimer where the belt hit the wrong person.

⑥ In terms of defences, Abdul may try to rely on duress of circumstances as in the case of Willer. In the case of Martin, it was held that the defence was only available if the defendant was acting to avoid a threat of death or grievous bodily harm to himself or others and another reasonable person would have done the same. This could be used as the frying pan was a threat to him and another person would probably have done the same.

Examiner commentary

① A nice opening statement where Seren has outlined the relevant statutory provisions. She also does well to state that a person could be charged with one offence but plea bargain to another and she will therefore consider a range of potential offences. This is a good approach.

② The key with the non-fatal offences is to deal with each offence separately, outlining the actus reus and mens rea of each offence and including case law where appropriate then applying the law to the facts of the scenario. This is the approach that Seren has taken here and she has defined the elements of s.20 GBH and applied them to the facts to reach a conclusion. She has also given some background on the offence of GBH stating that it is triable either way and the maximum sentence.

③ Another very good paragraph that follows the format used in the one above. She has correctly identified that they could plea bargain between offences and a person could be charged with either GBH or ABH. She has included more relevant case law here and

dealt with the two aspects of ABH very well (first an assault or battery and second the actual bodily harm).

④ It is also a preferable approach with a problem question on non-fatal offences to deal with each person separately. Here, Seren has logically moved on to consider the injury sustained by Ken from fainting. She has again identified and applied the elements of both assault (which she discounted) and battery which was more likely. She also did well to pick up that the battery could be indirectly applied. More good case law cited. One point to note is that Seren has not yet considered any defences which are required for this question. The preferable approach would be to highlight any relevant defences for each 'incident' that has taken place. Seren has chosen to leave a discussion of defences until the end but she may run out of time.

⑤ Very good identification of the doctrine of transferred malice and case of Latimer. This was an important point to pick up on that weaker students would have missed.

⑥ Seren finally gets on to defences which are important for this question. She correctly identifies one potential but then her answer stops abruptly. There were other defences to consider such as necessity for Abdul and possibly self defence for Ken. It would appear that Seren was running low on time to stop so quickly and the lack of discussion on the other defences means her mark is capped at bottom 'sound'.

Mark awarded:
AO2 – 11
AO3 – 1
Total = 12 out of 14 (86% Grade A)

This is a sound answer despite the lack of depth on defences. It is important to remember with non-fatal scenario questions that a discussion of the actus reus, mens rea and case law is required for each offence considered. Seren has used this logical approach and correctly said that it is unclear sometimes which offence the defendant will be charged with, hence the need to consider more than one. To achieve top marks, she needed more depth on the other defences available.

---

b) Explain how a jury would be selected if Abdul were to be tried in the Crown Court. *(11 marks)*

Tom's answer: Grade D

① The Crown court consists of 12 jury members. Jurors are lay people who represent society. Their role is to decide a verdict of guilty or not guilty. They do not decide the sentence.

② Under the Juries Act 1974 it highlights the qualifications for a juror. Firstly a juror must be aged between 18 and 70. These persons must be on the electoral register and they are selected at random. Next an eligible candidate for jury service must have a fixed address and must have residency in the UK for 5 years since their 13th birthday. Next prior to the Criminal Justice Act 2003 (CJA 2003) lawyers, judges, doctors and police were not eligible to serve as jurors. However, now these professions are able to be selected for jury service.

③ Also under the CJA 2003, it states that persons with mental disabilities are ineligible for jury service.

④ This shows the spectrum of eligible people who are able to sit as a juror. Once selected, a juror can be removed from the panel if they have a connection with the defendant or the victim.

⑤ In summary, this highlights the selection of people for jury service if Abdul's case goes to the Crown court.

Examiner commentary

① Good to see an introduction even if it is brief. Tom has correctly identified the jury's role in the Crown court and their role in delivering a verdict but not the sentence. He could also state that they try questions of fact and the judge tries questions of law.

② Tom has done well to correctly highlight the qualifications of jurors but needed to cite the Criminal Justice Act 2003 at the beginning, which provides the new selection criteria and amended the Juries Act 1974. He does well to then realise that the CJA 2003 is relevant in terms of allowing some who used to be ineligible to now serve as jurors.

③ A short paragraph but correct. He has identified the remaining category of ineligibility. He could also have brought in here some detail on who is disqualified from jury service.

④ This would have been an ideal opportunity for a discussion of the procedure for selection and the role of the Central Juror Summoning Bureau. He should also have considered the vetting of jurors and challenges that can be made perhaps including some cases to illustrate. This question was quite narrow and so it was important to include everything that was relevant in order to achieve the marks available.

⑤ A limited conclusion that doesn't really say much of any value.

Mark awarded:
AO1 – 5
AO3 – 1
Total = 6 out of 11 (55% Grade D)

This is a top limited answer thereby only allowing Tom to achieve the 1 mark for communication. He touches upon many key areas but his answer lacks breadth and explanation. He does well to include the relevant statutes and show a limited understanding of the changes made as a result of the CJA. He needed more on the procedure for selection of jurors and

consideration of some wider issues such as vetting and juror challenge, which were relevant to the question posed. It wouldn't have taken much extra to push Tom into the adequate boundary which would then usually allow him to gain the two AO3 marks for communication thereby increasing his mark further still.

Seren's answer: Grade A

① Juries are used in the Crown Court as a way of deciding guilt or innocence. Juries account for less than 2% of criminal cases as they are only used in the Crown Court where a defendant pleads not guilty and 95% of criminal cases are tried in a Magistrates' Court.

② Originally juries were used for providing local knowledge and information, acting more as witnesses than decision makers. By the middle of the 15th century, juries assumed their modern role as deciders of fact. The judge decides questions of law.

③ Jury qualifications are set out in the Juries Act 1974 as amended by the Criminal Justice Act 2003. A person must be:
- aged 18–70
- on the electoral register
- resident in the UK, Channel Islands or Isle of Man for at least 5 years since the age of 13
- not disqualified
- not mentally disordered.

④ Before the Criminal Justice Act 2003, police, judges, solicitors, etc., could not sit as jurors but this was changed and now the only people not eligible are the mentally ill. The jury has become more representative as a result. Members of the armed forces are the only ones who can be automatically excused now, whereas before the CJA 2003, doctors, etc., could be excused as of right. Generally people should perform their jury service but it can be deferred if you have a holiday or wedding, for example, booked and it can't be changed.

⑤ The role of the jury is to deliver a verdict of guilty or not guilty. In the Crown Court there are usually 12 members and at least 10 have to be in agreement of a verdict to uphold beyond reasonable doubt.

⑥ Juries are criticised as not being able to understand what is going on in the trial. Other criticisms are reflected in the fact that jury selection is random. It is done by computer at the Central Juror Summoning Bureau and can be a completely random selection. It could be all women or men or no ethnic minorities. In the case of Ford it was held there is no guarantee for an ethnic minority jury so there could be an unrepresentative sample selected which could be unfair.

Examiner commentary

① A good introduction to put the answer in context. This is a question about the selection of jurors in criminal cases and so, Seren is correct to comment on their presence in the Crown Court.

② Seren has provided some background information here, though this is not strictly relevant to the question. Good mention of the fact that jurors decide questions of fact and judges questions of law.

③ This is the main focus of the question and Seren has correctly outlined the selection criteria under the Juries Act 1974 as amended. Good use of relevant and correct legal terminology here.

④ Seren has provided additional evaluation here still focused on the question. She has evaluated the selection criteria prior to the CJA 2003 and why these changes were made. She has also included detail about excusal as of right and the changes made to this.

⑤ Seren has progressed well here to consider the jury's role in the Crown Court and she has brought in the standard of proof. Good wider information here.

⑥ The question asks about the selection of jurors and the role of the Central Juror Summoning Bureau is important. It would also have been good to see Seren include detail on the procedure for selection and also jury vetting and challenge. All of these aspects are relevant to the particular question asked. She has done well to include the Ford case and evaluated this well but representativeness was not the main focus of the question.

Mark awarded:
AO1 – 7
AO3 – 2
Total = 9 out of 11 (82% Grade A)

This is a top adequate answer where Seren has focused on the question posed but provided some wider information, too, as the question was quite narrow. She has dealt with the changes to the selection of jurors well and correctly cited the relevant statutory provisions. She has included a good range of accurate legal authority and shown her understanding of the jury in general. Good use of the Ford case that enhances her answer and focuses on the issue of selection and representation. In order for her answer to be a sound one, she needed a little more on the selection procedure and also vetting and challenge to jurors. With limited time, it is important to use it wisely and include those aspects most relevant to answering the question posed.

3. LA3 Police Powers

Study the text below and answer the questions based on it.

Oscar was arrested for aggravated burglary and taken to his local police station, which was short-staffed due to a flu epidemic. There was no one available to act as a custody officer, and no custody record was opened for him. Oscar asked to speak to his lawyer, but was told by his arresting officer that he did not have the time to ring him. Oscar's request to have his wife informed was also turned down. Oscar was placed in a cell without food and water, and left there for 37 hours before being collected for interview. On his way to the interview room he began to feel sick, and asked to see a doctor and a lawyer. The interviewing officer agreed, on condition that Oscar admit the offence. Oscar reluctantly agreed to sign a confession. Shortly after this, Harold, a duty solicitor, arrived to advise Oscar.

a) In the light of reported case law and other sources of law, consider whether Oscar's rights as a detainee were respected during his time in police custody. *(14 marks)*

Tom's answer: Grade D

① I have been asked to consider whether Oscar's rights as a detainee were respected during his time in police custody. The rights to do with the police are found in the Police and Criminal Evidence Act from now on called PACE. There are also Codes of Practice. Many statutes regarding the police have also been passed such as the Serious Organised Crime and Police Act 2005 from now on called SOCPA.

② To start off, the police could have stopped and searched Oscar. This can be found in sections 1–7 of PACE and Code A. The first point to look at is the arrest of Oscar. This is found in s.24 PACE as amended by SOCPA. The police officer should have told Oscar the reason for the arrest and cautioned him. They should then have taken him to the police station.

③ Oscar did ask to speak to his solicitor. Under s.58 of PACE, the suspect has the right to free legal advice. This request was rejected. Oscar also asked to have his wife informed of his arrest. s.56 PACE says that you have the right to have

someone informed of your arrest. Again this was turned down by the police. s.57 PACE says that anyone under the age of 17 or mentally disordered has the right to have an appropriate adult present during questioning. We are not told Oscar's age or if he is mentally disordered.

④ A person can only be questioned for so long. They must be given breaks. Also they have to be given food and drink and sleep if they need it. They also detained Oscar for too long and they kept him for 37 hours and they should only have detained him for 24 or 36 for an indictable offence. Code C tells the police that suspects should be kept in clean conditions with proper treatment and breaks as I have said above.

⑤ Confessions can be found in s.76 PACE and Oscar has been tricked into giving a confession. I don't believe this could be used in court as it would be very unfair.

In conclusion a number of rights as a detainee were rejected by the police and he can sue them for false imprisonment.

Examiner commentary

① Tom has done well to provide a brief introduction introducing the statutes that govern police powers. He has given the full titles of both PACE and SOCPA which is good. He has done well to identify the Codes of Practice but could have explained their use and effect a little more.

② With the new LA3 paper, the scenarios are a little shorter to account for the two-part questions. As a result and as with this question, part a) only deals with a few aspects of police powers. The question only required a discussion of the powers and rights of detainees from arrival at the police station. The stop and search and arrest were not relevant to this question. In this paragraph, Tom has discussed stop and search and arrest, both of which are not relevant to this question and did not carry any credit. His final sentence is where the application should begin and he needed to cite s.30 PACE for the requirement to take a suspect to the police station as soon as practicable after the arrest.

③ A good paragraph where Tom has correctly identified some key rights of suspects and applied them to the facts, which is crucial with the LA3 problem scenario questions. Good citation of correct legal authority. Tom has also included s.57, which, though not relevant to this scenario, has been dealt with appropriately by saying that more information is needed to correctly apply this section.

④ Tom has done well to identify Code C, though this is not explained very well. He also includes information about the detention periods but needs to cite the relevant sections of PACE (ss.40 and 41) and bring in the review of detention and custody record. He does, however, apply the law to the facts, which is important.

⑤ Good to see a mention, albeit brief, of s.76 and the admissibility of confession evidence. This is relevant to the scenario, though Tom should have included a definition of 'oppression' or 'unreliability' to expand this point and could have included s.78 regarding admissibility of evidence of any kind.

Mark awarded:
AO2 – 7
AO3 – 1
Total = 8 out of 14 (57% Grade D)
Though Tom has included some irrelevant parts in his answer, he does appreciate the need to apply the law that he has learnt to the facts of the scenario. This is key with LA3 questions. Citation of the relevant sections of PACE and other Acts can also make the difference between achieving the top and bottom of a mark boundary and/or moving to the next mark boundary. Tom has touched upon quite a range of relevant areas and has included some legal authority. However, there is not enough of a range or reference to specific sections of PACE to warrant the top of the 'adequate' boundary of marks. Tom also only mentions some sections/points without full explanation. A good basis and with a little more could have achieved the top of the 'adequate' boundary and taken his mark to a borderline C/B.

A2 Criminal Law and Justice: Study and Revision Guide

Seren's answer: Grade A

① It would appear that Oscar's rights as a detainee have not been respected during his time in police custody. The main act governing police powers is the Police and Criminal Evidence Act 1984 which from here on will be referred to as PACE. Attached to PACE are the Codes of Practice and within the codes are guidance notes on the exercise of police powers. The Code that applies to police station procedure is Code C which will be discussed later.

② On arrival at the police station, Oscar should have been taken to see the custody officer. We are told that no one was available which is a breach. Every designated police station (one that has holding facilities) should have a custody officer according to s.36 PACE. If a custody officer is not available, as in this case, a sergeant or above can act as a custody officer, and even a constable can act temporarily as a custody officer. He has to remain independent. Under s.37, the custody officer decides whether to detain the suspect if they have reasonable suspicion that the suspect has committed an offence. If there is enough evidence to charge the suspect, then he should be charged immediately. However the custody officer may authorise continued detention where there are reasonable grounds for believing that this is necessary to secure or preserve evidence, or where the custody officer has reasonable grounds to believe that it is necessary to obtain evidence by questioning the suspect.

③ We are told that Oscar is taken to his local police station, which presumably is as soon as practicable under PACE s.30 unless he is needed at the scene. As there is no custody officer, it can be assumed that no custody record was opened for him which is a breach of Code C.

④ Oscar asked to speak to his lawyer but was told there wasn't enough time to ring him. Certain information must be given to the suspect immediately under Code C – the right to have someone informed of the arrest under s.56, the right to legal advice under s.58, and the right to consult the Codes of Practice, which must be kept at every police station. Therefore, Oscar should have been provided with information about these and allowed to see his lawyer before questioning started. This is also a breach of art 6 of the European Convention on Human Rights, the right to a fair trial. They are not respecting Oscar's rights as a detainee. He was also denied to contact his wife which is a breach. Suspects can be denied these rights to legal advice and to have someone informed for up to 36 hours where the offence is an indictable one and where it is suspected that evidence or witnesses will be tampered with. There are some important cases that confirm that suspects are allowed to consult legal advice. In the case of R v Samuel his confession could not be used in court as he was denied access to legal advice and in R v Grant his conviction for murder was quashed as a result of being denied legal advice.

⑤ Oscar was placed in a cell without food or water which is a breach of Code C. This states the conditions of the detention (e.g. adequate lighting, heating and ventilation with breaks for meals and the toilet). There should also be breaks during questioning. Clearly these have been breached as Oscar was left in a cell and without food or water for 37 hours. This is not acceptable.

⑥ Oscar was then told he could see a lawyer and a doctor if he confessed which he did. Under s.76 PACE, a confession that has been obtained by oppression (which is defined in s.76(2) as any inhumane or degrading treatment) or in any circumstances that would render the confession unreliable, will be inadmissible in the trial. It is arguable that Oscar's confession was obtained thought inhumane treatment by leaving him in a cell and without food or water for 37 hours.

⑦ The time that Oscar was detained was also a breach of PACE s.41. Suspects can be detained for 36 hours for an indictable offence following SOCPA 2005 (24 hours otherwise). Their detention should be reviewed after the first 6 hours and then at intervals of no more than 9 hours according to s.40 PACE. There is no mention of this review of Oscar's detention and as he has been left in a cell for 37 hours, it is a clear breach of s.41 and s.40. His interview should also have been tape recorded under s.60.

⑧ It would appear that several of Oscar's rights haven't been respected. They were also not explained to him, which is required under PACE. He can make a complaint to the IPCC, get his confession excluded and may also be able to claim damages.

Examiner commentary

① A very good opening statement putting the answer in context by citing the relevant statute and Codes of Practice. Seren has done well to give the full title of the Act but make it clear that from thereon it will be referred to as PACE. This is fine as it shows the examiner that she knows the full title and will save time by referring to it's abbreviated title from thereon.

② A very good paragraph where she demonstrates her knowledge and understanding of the role of the custody officer. She has done well to correctly refer to the relevant sections of PACE and has given a very good level of depth regarding continued detention. She has also used key legal terms accurately and confidently here.

③ Perhaps an afterthought to mention s.30 which would have been more relevant to begin with but still relevant. Seren has also mentioned the custody record.

④ Further accurate citation of relevant sections of PACE here. Seren has discussed s.56 and s.58 which are crucial to this question. She has done particularly well to recognise that these rights can be deferred for 36 hours in serious cases. She has also done well to refer to a couple of key cases which confirmed the importance of the right to legal advice.

⑤ Seren is working logically through the issues and probably the best approach is to deal with the facts as they are presented (chronologically). She has moved on to consider the detention and the conditions of detention guided by Code C. She could also have mentioned the fact that breach of the codes of practice has to be serious and substantial in order for evidence to be considered for exclusion.

⑥ Very good progression here on to the question of admissibility of evidence as per s.76 and s.78. This is an important aspect of the question as it explores the implications of the breaches of police powers and the likelihood of evidence being inadmissible due to the breaches.

⑦ Seren has again included a good range of specific and relevant section numbers. Here she has commented on the detention period and the review that should have taken place. Throughout her answer she is applying the law to the facts, which is essential with a legal problem scenario.

⑧ A good, albeit brief conclusion to focus on the question but also to include some wider information about the remedies available for Oscar following his treatment. Though not strictly relevant to the question, it rounds off her answer nicely and shows breadth of understanding.

Mark awarded:
AO2 – 13
AO3 – 1
Total = 14 out of 14 (100% Grade A)

This is a top, sound answer and fully warrants the 100% mark awarded. Seren has worked logically through the potential breaches of police powers and accurately cited a mixture of legal authority to substantiate her application. She has done more than just describe the powers but has applied the powers to the facts of the scenario, which is essential for LA3 problem style questions. Some students fall into the trap of merely outlining the range of powers and responsibilities the police have, which limits the marks available to them. Seren, however, has correctly and soundly applied the law to the scenario – a very good answer.

b) Describe the sources of legal advice and assistance that may be available to Oscar. *(11 marks)*

Tom's answer: Grade D

① It is important that everyone should have access to justice. It is considered to be a fundamental principle of society. It is a person's right under art 6 ECHR. This gives the right to a fair trial.

② The legal services commission oversees the criminal defence fund which is a demand-led service so anyone who fits the tests will be allowed funding. In this case, Oscar would have the right to free legal advice under s.58 of PACE. He could have a duty solicitor at the police station who can be called out at any time of the day or night.

③ Legal aid will be given if it is felt that the defendant is likely to lose his liberty or livelihood. In this case it would probably be allowed as it is aggravated burglary and so likely to result in a prison sentence. Also if a person has over a certain amount of money or assets they may have to make a contribution to the legal aid. We are not told how much Oscar earns or has, so I can't advise properly here.

④ Also depending on where Oscar lives, he may qualify for a public defender. It is only a pilot so is only available in some areas and we are not told where Oscar lives.

⑤ As you can see, Oscar has quite a few options available and I need some more information to be able to advise properly.

Examiner commentary

① A brief introduction but puts the answer in context. Tom has included the right to a fair trial under art 6 ECHR. This is relevant, though he should also have included the Legal Services Commission as overseeing legal aid to be more specific.

② Tom has included some important information here but should specifically mention the Criminal Defence Service rather than merely the fund. He also does well to say it is demand led but needs to include that it is administered by the Legal Services Commission established following the Access to Justice Act 1999. He has correctly included s.58 and the right to legal advice at the police station though could also have discussed the availability of a duty solicitor at the Magistrates' Court.

③ Tom seems to be talking about the means and merits tests here, though needs to make his points more explicitly and concisely using the appropriate legal terminology.

④ Good mention of public defenders though this again should have been expanded some more. He also needed to include information about the Legal Services Commission and quality marks.

⑤ Tom is perhaps running out of ideas here and makes a general statement about needing more information to advise properly and Oscar having several options. He needs to be a lot more specific in his conclusion.

Mark awarded:
AO1 – 5
AO3 – 1
Total = 6 out of 11 (55% Grade D)

An upper 'limited' answer. Tom has touched upon several relevant areas but rarely offers depth of explanation. He also fails to include some fundamental areas such as the Legal Services Commission and the Access to Justice Act. His answer lacks specificity and, though showing a general understanding of the area, is limited in his description.

Seren's answer: Grade A

① At the time of arrival at the police station it is the custody officer's duty to ensure a poster of available rights is available for the defendant to look at. This is a requirement under Code C. It is the job of the custody officer to inform Oscar that legal advice is available privately and free of charge. There is a duty solicitor scheme in the police station which under PACE s.58, every person arrested on suspicion of a crime has the right to free legal advice, either in person or over the telephone.

② Following the Access to Justice Act 1999, the Legal Services Commission was divided into two parts – the Community Legal Service and the Criminal Defence Service. The one needed here is the CDS. The CDS has duty solicitors available to give advice in the police station but they are also available at the Magistrates' Court and are available 24 hours a day. A duty solicitor must be LSC approved and have met the quality mark to ensure the standard of advice is good.

③ In some areas there is a lack of duty solicitors containing this quality marks. In some other areas there are public defenders who are defence lawyers employed by the Legal Service Commission. Public defenders and duty solicitors are free initially. There is no fixed budget for criminal legal aid as it is impossible to predict the amount of criminals needing representation each year and they can't be denied legal advice but to qualify for funding a defendant must pass two tests. First, the interests of justice test (or merits test) where they look If there is a risk of the defendant losing his liberty, damage to reputation, case involves an important question of law, etc. They also apply the means test which looks at the income and savings of the defendant.

④ Oscar would also be able to obtain legal advice from organisations such as the Citizens Advice Bureau and Law Centres where they give general advice and assistance.

Examiner commentary

① Seren has begun her answer by reiterating the rights of detainees to legal advice privately and free of charge and the requirements placed on custody officers to ensure access to these rights. Good citation of correct legal authority here.

② Seren has progressed logically on to the Legal Services Commission and their role following the Access to Justice Act 1999. Seren has included good reference to specific key concepts and legal authority to support. Her explanation is also 'sound' recognising the role of duty solicitors at Magistrates' Court as well as at police stations.

③ Lots of important information is contained in this paragraph. Seren has done well to include both a range and good explanation of these key points. Her work is more than merely descriptive. She has used key terms correctly such as means and merits tests and quality mark. She also touches upon the role of public defenders.

④ She brings in other ways of obtaining legal advice here which shows knowledge and understanding, though these are not really relevant to criminal law. Her work does lack a conclusion which is disappointing but this is reflected in the mark being at the bottom of the 'sound' category.

Mark awarded:
AO1 – 8
AO3 – 2
Total = 10 out of 11 (91% Grade A)

Seren has done well with this synoptic question. She has discussed a good range of issues and been detailed in her explanation and reference to key areas such as the **Access to Justice Act and Criminal Defence Service**. She also works logically through the issues from the detention and also brings in Oscar to link it back to the scenario. Students always struggle with the synoptic questions and legal aid is always a popular exam question. Make sure you also revise civil legal aid even though this is a criminal paper as it could just as likely come up!

4. LA3 Homicide

Study the text below and answer the questions based on it.

Late one evening, Debbie went to the lane at the back of some houses and climbed up a drainpipe, intending to enter what she thought was her boyfriend's bedroom window, and climbed in. Unfortunately, she had chosen the wrong house, and had entered the bedroom of her boyfriend's next door neighbour, George, who was asleep in bed. George woke up and began screaming. Debbie panicked and put her hand over George's mouth, which caused George to faint with fright. Debbie was convinced that she had accidentally killed him, and decided to dispose of his body. She managed to drag George out to her car, drove to a nearby river, and threw him in. The shock of the cold water caused George to regain consciousness, and he began to swim. However, a passing boat under the command of its drunken captain, James, hit George and knocked him unconscious again. George drowned. Debbie was later arrested in connection with the death of George.

a) In the light of reported case law and other sources of law, consider whether Debbie may be criminally liable for George's death. *(14 marks)*

Tom's answer: Grade D

① When assessing whether a person is liable for a death they must have both the actus reus and the mens rea of the crime. The death was of a human being as the offence was against somebody who could function outside of their mother's body.

② A person has to be the main cause of the person's death. This leads to the chain of causation needing to be assessed. There are two types of causation that have to be proven: factual and legal. Factual causation has two parts to it: this is the but for test and the de minimis test. In this case, Debbie could have liability for the death as if it wasn't for her actions then he would not have been hit by the boat. However, when we look at the de minimis rule, we have to ask whether she was the main cause of death. In this case, she was not; the main cause was the boat hitting George.

③ Legal causation has three parts to it which are the operative and significant cause which when assessing cases such as R v Cheshire, R v Smith and R v Jordan and referring it to this case it has been proven that George's death was not caused by Debbie's actions because he got hit by a boat which shows that he clearly broke the chain of causation. The act was also not reasonably foreseeable as it is very unlikely that if a reasonable and sober person dumped someone into a river

that a boat would kill them. The opposite was shown in R v Pagett and R v Corbett.

④ When looking at the mens rea, the person would refer to the Nedrick test as it was indirect intention. This is where there was a virtual certainty that the death would occur as a result of the defendant's actions. This was amended by Woolin and the words were changed from 'inflict' to 'find' intention. As the virtual certainty test would not be satisfied, we should consider reducing the charge of murder to manslaughter.

⑤ Voluntary manslaughter is irrelevant because Debbie could not claim provocation as at no time was she provoked by George. She also cannot use diminished responsibility as she was not suffering from an abnormality of mind nor was it a suicide pact.

⑥ However, there are two other types of manslaughter which are unlawful manslaughter and gross negligence manslaughter. Unlawful act manslaughter is applied where a person has the actus reus for a crime but they will not have the mens rea for the murder, but just of the lesser crime. To prove unlawful act manslaughter they must have committed an unlawful act. The leading case is R v Church which laid down a two-part test. Did the person realise that their actions would cause the death and would the reasonable person have foreseen that they would have caused the death.

Examiner commentary

① This is very typical of a homicide answer; the candidate does not explain what the actus reus and mens rea of the offence actually are. It is a bad habit to launch straight into causation; he needs to explain the elements of the offence before discussing them. A useful definition for murder comes from Lord Justice Coke.

② A good explanation of the factual causation tests here, but there is a lack of case law. An obvious choice to support the but for test would be R v White, and for the de minimis rule a common citation is R v Pagett. There is a vague application here of factual causation, and this lack of substance and supporting authority will affect Tom's mark.

③ It is good to see that Tom has knowledge of some of the elements of legal causation here; the operative and substantive cause of death is discussed in detail with some supporting authority, as is the reasonable foreseeability test, though R v Roberts is also a useful case to discuss the concept of foreseeability. Tom

should also discuss the thin skull test and use R v Blaue as a supporting citation. It is imperative that ALL elements of the offence are discussed throughout, even if it they do not apply to the scenario, you have to make this clear to the examiner.

④ Excellent use of case law here, the mens rea of homicide is a tricky area in which to score highly. To improve the quality of this, Tom could have also discussed the requirement of coincidence of actus reus and mens rea, as illustrated in cases such as Thabo Meli, Le Brun and Church which highlighted that where a non-fatal offence carried out with *mens rea*, and the act which eventually causes death, are part of a single sequence of events, the elements of murder or manslaughter will be satisfied. This is especially so when the subsequent acts were designed to conceal the original non-fatal assault.

⑤ It is a needless exercise discussing voluntary manslaughter because it is evident it does not apply. However, Tom will not be penalised because the fact that he has ruled it out shows correct application of the law.

⑥ Here, Tom has identified that unlawful act manslaughter could apply to the scenario, but has not then applied the law to the scenario by identifying what the unlawful act would be, and supported it with relevant legal authority; there are plenty of examples, such as R v Lowe. There is an attempt to discuss the elements of constructive manslaughter, but it has not been applied to the scenario with any conviction. Further, Tom has omitted to consider the liability of James, the drunken captain, who could find himself liable for gross negligence manslaughter. Again, the elements of this crime should be discussed and applied to the scenario appropriately.

Mark awarded:
AO2 – 7
AO3 – 1
Total = 8 out of 14 (57% Grade D)

This is a well-structured answer, but there is a lack of legal authority and legal substance, which has affected the mark.

Seren's answer: Grade A

① For Debbie to be liable for George's death, she must have both the actus reus and the mens rea for murder. The actus reus for murder is to kill, which is legally recognised as the brain stem of a human being dead. This is why doctors lawfully turn off life support machines in cases such as Malcherek and Steel and Tony Bland. A human being is legally a human once they live independently of their mother; this was held in the Attorney General's Reference No 3. The mens rea is malice aforethought, which means intention to kill or intention to cause grievous bodily harm. Intention can be direct or indirect as seen in Moloney and in Nedrick where death would be a virtual certainty; however, it is clear that Debbie did not intend to kill or cause grievous bodily harm.

② Debbie must have caused the death and therefore factual causation shall be considered. The 'but for' test proposes that 'but for' Debbie's action would George have died as seen in R v White.

③ Legal causation should also be considered. Debbie was under the belief she had killed George and so tried to hide it by throwing him in a river. As seen in R v Smith, a substantial and operative break in the causation must free her from murder. The fact a boat had knocked him out provides a significant and operative factor. It was not foreseeable that this would happen, so therefore there may be a break in the chain of causation. Therefore, Debbie did not have the mens rea for murder so constructive manslaughter should be considered.

④ Unlawful and dangerous act manslaughter states that a person can be liable for murder if their unlawful actions caused the death of the victim. R v Lowe says that it cannot be due to omission and R v Franklin held that it must be an unlawful criminal act. In Franklin, the court held that the civil wrong of trespass was not enough to satisfy constructive manslaughter. Debbie had assaulted George under s.39 Criminal Justice Act 1988 by causing him to feel immediate fear that unlawful force was going to be applied. However, she did not have the intention or subjective recklessness and could not be

guilty of that. However, by putting her hand over his mouth, she has caused a battery under s.39 Criminal Justice Act 1988 and had the suitable mens rea for this of intention or subjective recklessness. This had caused George to faint which is actual bodily harm under s.47 Offences against the Person Act 1861. R v Donovan held that a loss of consciousness can amount to s.47 Offences against the Person Act 1861 and it was held no extra mens rea is needed to be liable for a s.47 offence as seen in Savage and Parmenter and therefore Debbie had caused an unlawful and dangerous act by causing ABH with the mens rea of battery.

⑤ Whether it was dangerous is addressed by R v Church test, which states that a sober and reasonable person would be liable for a death if they recognise some harm might occur, albeit not serious harm. Similar to the case of R v Church, Debbie had thrown the body in the river. It is an objective test so it was held to be irrelevant whether she honestly and genuinely believed he was dead, she would still be liable when George actually drowned. The courts are deemed to have the same information as the defendant and no more and therefore this is purely objective which could see Debbie being liable for George's death.

⑥ However, it may be reasonably unforeseeable that a boat would come and knock and kill George and so it could break the chain of causation. It may be possible that James who is a captain owes a duty of care to George and he had breached this duty of care to cause the death. This is gross negligence manslaughter where the person has acted so manifestly wrong that no amount of compensation will suffice. As James was drunk and owed a duty of care to act responsibly, he may have caused the death and so Debbie would not be liable.

⑦ It is unlikely that Debbie would be convicted of murder as she did not have the mens rea of malice aforethought. It appears more likely that she will be liable for constructive manslaughter as she had caused both an unlawful and dangerous act and a mistake is irrelevant as it is an objective test.

Examiner commentary

① An outstanding introductory paragraph – Seren has immediately made it clear that she understands the concept of murder and its elements, and has a very detailed knowledge of legal authority. This type of explanation is always missing from candidates' answers and Seren has done well to provide this detail. This is an almost flawless introduction and would be a useful one to learn and can be recited in any answer on homicide.

② Immediately, Seren launches into application of the law to the scenario, using factual causation as a starting point = the 'but for' test is correctly applied with relevant legal authority. This would have been further enhanced by discussion of the 'de minimis' rule with supporting case law.

③ Legal causation is correctly applied by Seren in this paragraph, also with relevant legal authority. An almost flawless application could have been further enhanced with a mention of the thin skull rule (R v Blaue), but this does not directly apply to the scenario so Seren will not be penalised.

④ This section has scored Seren a lot of marks because she has recognised the presence of unlawful and dangerous act manslaughter, or constructive manslaughter as it is sometimes referred to. There is excellent application of the offence – all elements are stated and applied and importantly the unlawful act – s.39 Criminal Justice Act 1989 and s.47 Offences Against the Person Act 1861 has been correctly identified. All legal terminology is used correctly and Seren has obviously understood and applied the offence.

⑤ Seren continues to apply the elements of constructive manslaughter, and good citation of R v Church, but there are more cases that could be used to support the actus reus of this offence; particularly R v Dawson and R v Watson. Candidates who fail to correctly identify offences in a problem question scenario are likely to find themselves in a lower mark band because it demonstrates no more than a 'limited' application of the law. In Seren's answer, the correct identification of an offence and supporting authority clearly shows a 'sound' knowledge and application.

⑥ Seren here has also discussed the possibility of James being convicted of gross negligence manslaughter. This is demonstrative of an articulate, well thought out answer and attention to detail. There is a lack of supporting case law, such as Donoghue v Stevenson, but this can be forgiven because the recognition of this subtle addition to the scenario is commendable.

⑦ Seren has produced a rounded conclusion, which gives the examiner an 'answer' to the question as to for which offences Debbie may find herself liable. It is always good practice in a conclusion to identify the defendants and the potential offences that have been committed.

Mark awarded:
AO2 – 13
AO3 – 1
Total = 14 out of 14 (100% Grade A)

A very well-structured answer, with a logical approach to all elements of the relevant offences and, importantly supporting legal authority. Candidates should be prepared to recognise one or more of the following in a problem question on homicide:

- **Murder**
- **Voluntary manslaughter (usually diminished responsibility or loss of control)**
- **Involuntary manslaughter – constructive manslaughter**
- **Involuntary manslaughter – gross negligence manslaughter.**

---

b) Explain the powers of the police to grant bail   *(11 marks)*

Tom's answer: Grade D

① The police will arrest a person and they will be taken to the police station. They will be taken straight to the custody officer who will assess whether there is enough evidence to charge the suspect. They will either charge or grant bail. The police have to be careful when granting bail as under s4 of the Bail Act 1976 everyone is presumed to have the right to bail.

② There are reasons for bail not to be granted such as the address or name of the person is unknown, if they believe that the person has given a false name or address or if they believe the person is likely to commit another offence.

③ The reasons they do not like to hold people is because not giving bail can cause a loss of employment, they cannot speak to a their legal advisers properly and are more likely to plead guilty. All of these factors go against the person and in favour of the police.

④ Where a person has been arrested under a warrant the decision has effectively been made by the Magistrates as the warrant will state whether the person has been granted bail or not. There is also street bail where the police have the power to stop and charge a person in the street. They will issue all the paperwork at the point on the street which will later be entered in the police station and the person is under a duty to attend the police station at a given time. This means that they do not have to hold the suspect.

⑤ When a person is not given bail and is held in custody they must be brought before the Magistrates as soon as is practicable.

Examiner commentary

(1) (2) A basic outline of criminal procedure and where bail fits in relation to the police; however, this is quite basic, and there should be a lot more detail in relation to the police powers, since this is essentially what the question is asking. A major omission is s.38 Police and Criminal Evidence Act 1984 where the police powers to grant bail are found. Tom does go on to explain the circumstances under which the police can refuse bail, which is encouraging. Tom does well to reference The Bail Act 1976, particularly the presumption in favour of bail. Though again, there could be a reference to Article 5 ECHR – right to liberty which is a massive consideration when deciding whether bail should be granted.

(3) A good evaluation here of the positive aspects of granting bail, but there is not enough information on bail, and no reference to any statute provisions. This will greatly

affect Tom's mark and prevent him from entering the higher mark bands. There should be reference here to the exceptions to granting bail, which centre around whether the police have substantial grounds for believing that the defendant, if released, would commit another offence, interfere with witnesses or fail to surrender to custody. Further, Tom should mention that the Criminal Justice and Public Order Act 1994 allows for the police to grant conditional bail – examples of such conditions would further enhance this answer.

(4) This paragraph is very credible; Tom makes reference to street bail, though again he is lacking in legal authority – s.4 Criminal Justice Act 2003 would be the relevant citation. However, he has to be credited with the attempt at explanation and evaluation of this relatively new concept of bail.

(5) A good reference to the consequences of the police refusing bail; however, this answer seems to come to an abrupt end.

It is good practice to round off the answer with a suitable conclusion and in such synoptic questions it is always a good idea to apply the law to the scenario that has been addressed in part a). Thus, Tom would give an indication whether Debbie would be able to receive bail or not. This is obviously going to be very hypothetical, but does show a willingness to apply the law to a given scenario.

Mark awarded:
AO1 – 5
AO3 – 1
Total = 6 out of 11 (55% Grade D)

There is a lot missing from this answer which is reflected in the relatively low mark that has been awarded. At this level, it is expected that candidates can cite all relevant legal authority and be able to provide a full and detailed explanation of the law.

Seren's answer: Grade A

(1) After arrest, under s.37 of the Police and Criminal Evidence Act 1984, a suspect should be brought before a custody officer who will decide if there is enough evidence to charge. Once charged under section s.38 a person should be given bail unless there are reasons why they should not. Reasons could include that they believe the name and address given is false, giving bail may cause harm to himself or others, or if there are substantial grounds for believing that they may interfere with witnesses or otherwise obstruct the course of justice or they would be likely to reoffend. A large number of offences are committed by people who are on bail for another offence.

(2) The Bail Act 1976 states under s.4 that there is a presumption bail should be given and this is in line with the principle of innocent until proven guilty and Article 5 ECHR right to liberty. They can be detained for up to 96 hours with the Magistrate's permission for effective investigation and further questioning. Usually, following the Criminal Justice Act 2003, they should be released after 24 hours.

(3) Under the Criminal Justice and Public Order Act 1994 the police can give conditional bail. This is where the suspect will be given bail on conditions such as not being able to go within a certain mile radius of the alleged offence or if they are likely to abscond they must surrender their passport or forfeit money. This is to ensure they turn up to the court date.

(4) The court will also consider certain factors when deciding whether or not to grant bail. Such factors include the nature and seriousness of the offence, the strength of the evidence, the community ties and character of the defendant, as well as the defendant's history of reporting to bail.

(5) Following the case of Cabellero, if a person has been arrested for an indictable offence, they should be allowed to apply for bail, which guarantees the suspect's human rights. However, it is only given in exceptional circumstances if they have served a prison sentence for murder, manslaughter or rape in the past. This is also contained in the Criminal Justice Act 2003.

Examiner commentary

(1) A flawless introduction covering all the relevant legal authority, by which the police are governed. A huge social issue is raised here; that there are a number of offences committed by people who are on bail for another offence. This is a huge issue and shows knowledge of the more in-depth concerns surrounding the granting of bail. Crucially here, there is no mention of what happens when the police refuse bail – that is, they have to get the defendant in front of the Magistrates at the earliest opportunity.

(2) Key provisions of The Bail Act 1976 are alluded to here, predominantly the presumption in favour of bail and of course the reference to Article 5 ECHR – right to liberty is highly commendable. The situations when bail can be granted are also omitted; remember do not be afraid to state the obvious and Seren could have alluded to the fact that the police can grant bail

whether the suspect has been charged with an offence or not. If this can be supported with real examples from the news, then this would again demonstrate a broad knowledge and willingness to explore wider issues.

(3) Another flawless paragraph with reference to key legal authority. The citation of statute provisions proves to the examiner that there is indeed a broad knowledge of the topic and will usually result in marks being placed in the top two mark bands. Also relevant here would be the powers of the police to grant street bail.

(4) (5) This paragraph is more relevant to court bail, but Seren will not be penalised because it strengthens what is already apparent; that she has an in-depth knowledge of the intricacies of bail. The more subtle provisions of bail are also discussed with the citation of Cabellero – to further enhance this aspect, Seren should cite all the provisions of the Criminal Justice Act 2003, which provide

caveats to the granting of bail in court. Such provisions include the granting of bail for defendants who are found in possession of Class A drugs, those who are accused of indictable offences when a custodial sentence for a similar offence has been served, and where the offence has been committed whilst on bail for another offence.

Mark awarded:
AO1 – 7
AO3 – 2
Total = 9 out of 11 (82% Grade A)

An excellent answer overall with all the key aspects referenced and explained with supporting legal authority – there are a few key aspects missing, but not enough to detract from the high quality of what has been written.

5. LA4 Section A General Defences

Evaluate the extent to which intoxication by alcohol and other drugs can be used as a defence to a criminal charge. *(25 marks)*

Tom's answer: Grade C

① There are two types of intoxication: voluntary intoxication and involuntary intoxication.

② Voluntary intoxication is where the defendant knows they are consuming the alcohol or drugs. Intoxication cannot be used for basic intent crimes; these are crimes such as GBH, assault, battery and ABH. However, voluntary intoxication cannot be used as a defence for specific intent crimes either, such as murder or rape because they cannot be committed recklessly.

③ Involuntary intoxication can be used as a defence for any crime. However, the defendant must prove that they were unaware of consuming the alcohol or drugs. This may be caused by prescribed drugs, calming drugs or laced drinks. For example, in the case of Hardie, the defendant and his wife had split up and because of this the defendant took his wife's prescribed drugs which caused him to set the bedroom on fire. He was not liable because he had no recollection of it happening.

④ There is also the case where the defendant and his girlfriend were taking drugs, and the defendant was hallucinating and caused him to kill his girlfriend. He was charged with

manslaughter. So as we can see by this case the defence of intoxication lowers the sentence for the defendant.

⑤ For voluntary intoxication to be used as a defence the mens rea must have been taken away, which means the defendant must be in such an intoxicated state that he/she cannot remember anything. However, we could argue that in Hardie where he took the drug of his wife, he intended to take the prescribed drug which caused him to set fire to the bedroom. Maybe if he hadn't taken the drug he wouldn't have committed the arson. Those who take prescribed drugs without realising their effects should have a defence because they were prescribed the drugs and there is no intention of becoming intoxicated. Those who do voluntarily intoxicate themselves should I believe not be allowed a defence because they have the intention to go out and get themselves intoxicated. Even if they have no mens rea, it is still their responsibility to look after themselves and control their behaviour.

⑥ In conclusion, the extent to which intoxication by alcohol and other drugs can be used as a defence to a criminal charge is limited depending on whether the intoxication is voluntary or involuntary.

Examiner commentary

① Tom begins by identifying and defining the main concepts required of the question. However, ideas are simplistic and undeveloped. It may be useful here to have expanded with a more sophisticated definition of intoxication and the effect of the defence if successful.

② Understanding the distinction and the different effects of the defence between voluntary and involuntary intoxication is certainly a good basis. Further, an understanding of basic and specific intent is key to providing a full answer to this question so Tom does well to make this reference. However, there are key cases missing here such as DPP v Majewski (1977), and more detail needs to be given on the effect of the defence on specific intent crimes; i.e. that the defendant will be charged with the corresponding lesser offence.

③ Good reference to relevant case law here; however, Tom is lacking substance here, in terms of talking about the necessary lack of mens rea for involuntary intoxication to be a defence. For more than a 'limited' knowledge it is expected that candidates demonstrate an understanding of how a defendant could become involuntarily intoxicated, with supporting case law, including R v Kingston, which gives us a distinction from R v Hardie.

④ There is an attempt at citation of the case of R v Lipman here, but it is very weak and vague. Again, Tom has neglected to discuss the relevance of the case in any detail, though there is an attempt where he says it lowers the sentence – what he is referring to is that the defendant will be charged with the corresponding lesser offence – e.g. murder to manslaughter.

⑤ This is a strong paragraph because Tom hints at understanding the need for lack of mens rea. There is also a good attempt at some evaluative content, though this is not as strong as might be expected for a 'sound' evaluation.

⑥ A basic conclusion with no real substance or evaluation of the defence.

Mark awarded:
AO1 – 7
AO2 – 6
AO3 – 2
Total = 15 out of 25 (60% Grade C)

Tom's essay demonstrates some knowledge and understanding, arguably to an 'adequate' level, because many of the key concepts pertinent to the defence of intoxication are discussed. However, his skills are 'limited' because of the lack of case law and substantive evaluation.

Seren's answer: Grade A

① When a person is charged with an offence, there are many defences which may downgrade their charge, for example from murder to manslaughter. Intoxication is a defence applied when someone has either drunk alcohol or taken drugs. However, it cannot always be accepted as a defence and some people claim that it is not a real defence.

(2) Intoxication is used when a person cannot form the necessary mens rea for the offence. In the case of R v Kingston, the defendant went to his business colleague's house and so did a 15-year-old boy. The drinks were laced with drugs and when they were both intoxicated, Mr Kingston indecently assaulted the boy. He was initially attracted to young boys but he would not act on these tendencies. His business associates knew this and so did it on purpose and took a photograph in order to blackmail him. The House of Lords stated that a drunken intent is still intent and the defendant had the mens rea for the offence because he had a history of this behaviour, therefore this shows that even if you have been involuntarily intoxicated then you cannot always use the defence.

(3) When a person has committed an offence the court has to decide whether the offence was one of specific or basic intent. Specific intent crimes are when the mens rea is that of intention, and basic intent crimes are when the mens rea is recklessness. Specific intent crimes can normally use the defence of intoxication, whereas basic intent crimes cannot. This is seen in the case of Attorney General for Northern Ireland v Gallagher. Gallagher had spent 24 hours drinking and taking drugs and he then smashed a window and assaulted a police officer. He argued that he could not remember anything and so did not have the necessary mens rea for the offence. However, on appeal the House of Lords did not allow intoxication because the crimes that Gallagher committed were basic intent crimes. Therefore, this shows that intoxication is used in specific intent crimes but not basic intent crimes. The leading case which shows that intoxication cannot be used for basic intent crimes is DPP v Majewski where the defendants had been drinking for 24 hours and caused criminal damage and assaulted a police officer.

(4) However, intoxication can be used in both specific and basic intent crimes if the defendant has been intoxicated involuntarily and had no mens rea. Intoxication is not used when people do not realise what they are taking. For instance, in the case of Allen, the defendant was unaware of the alcohol content present in the wine he was drinking. It can also not be used when people voluntarily take drugs. For instance, in the case of R v Hardie, a man had an argument with his girlfriend and they had split up. In order to calm himself, he took Valium, which was prescribed for his girlfriend. He then set the room on fire when his girlfriend and daughter were downstairs in the living room. He was charged with the offence of damaging property and putting the lives of two people at risk. He tried to argue intoxication but he was not allowed to use it because his mens rea was recklessness; it was reckless to take those drugs.

(5) In the case of R v Irwin and Richardson students threw one of their fellow students off the balcony. This included the defence of intoxication since they were all drunk. Also in the case of R v Lipman, the defendant had taken a drug and the jury tried to argue whether or not he would have committed the offence if he had been sober and it was unlikely he would have. The case involved stuffing a sheet down his girlfriend's mouth which choked her to death. Therefore, in some cases, intoxication can be used, especially for specific intent offences.

(6) Intoxication cannot be used where there is a case of 'dutch courage'. This means drinking on purpose so that when they commit the offence they do not have the necessary intent. If intoxication was allowed in these cases then a lot more people would be doing this to excuse crimes. This is shown in the case of Attorney General for Northern Ireland v Gallagher where the defendant wanted to kill his wife. He bought a knife and a bottle of whisky; drank the whisky and used the knife to stab her. Intoxication was not used here because he had the mens rea whilst sober.

(7) In the case of R v O'Grady, the defendant was voluntarily intoxicated and then he murdered his friend because he thought his friend was going to kill him. You could argue intoxication here because he had made a mistake. However, mistake cannot be used as a defence when intoxicated. For instance, a case involving a rapist; if he got drunk and raped a girl then he would not be able to argue mistake since he had voluntarily become intoxicated.

(8) Some people might argue that it is not allowed and this is seen in the way suggestions for reform have been proposed. The first reform is codification, this sets out more information about the distinction between specific intent crimes and basic intent crimes. However, people argue that although the terminology is different, it is still unclear. A few years ago, the Law Commission proposed introducing a new offence, this was dangerous intoxication. This meant that if a person had involuntarily taken drugs or drunk alcohol but had the mens rea to commit the offence, then they could use the defence of dangerous intoxication. Other reforms include a special verdict and miscellaneous provisions. These reforms show that intoxication is not really a good defence since it is used in some offences and not others.

(9) However, this leads me to another reform that may have been introduced and that is to have intoxication as a defence for just specific intent crimes. Therefore in conclusion there are cases which can use intoxication as a defence, like in specific intent crimes. However, it is not really used in basic intent crimes. The ideas for reform show that it may not be a good defence; however, it is still used in certain situations when it comes to charging the offender.

Examiner commentary

(1) This is an excellent introduction; which introduces the key issue in the question; the definition of intoxication. Candidates should learn a well-rehearsed introduction to topics as it is the introduction that tends to be the most 'waffly' part of the answer.

(2) There is implication of an understanding of the core element of the defence; that is despite being intoxicated, did the defendant have the required mens rea? Seren has made this clear by immediately using a very relevant case. Mention of the difference between voluntary and involuntary intoxication would have added clarity.

(3) A vital distinction to make in any answer on intoxication; that of specific and basic intent; again with ample legal authority to support the explanations. Again, missing is the simple explanation of terms; here it

would have been appropriate to maybe give examples of specific and basic intent crimes. What is important, however, is that Seren has answered the question and explained how the defence can be used with specific and basic intent crimes.

(4) Involuntary intoxication is discussed in this paragraph, again with supporting legal authority. Two distinguishing cases are thoroughly explained. What Seren has done particularly well is discuss the facts of the case in a concise, succinct manner and explain the relevance of the case without copiously reciting too much irrelevant information.

(5) (6) There is ample legal authority used here to provide a detailed and thorough explanation of the caveats to the defence.

(7) The concept of drunken mistake is discussed here with the leading case of R v O'Grady; again Seren has done well to explore the

limitations of the defence, which will have scored her highly in the AO2 Assessment Objective where the examiner is looking for skills of evaluation and application.

(8) (9) A good consideration of proposals for reform; it is always advisable where necessary to discuss reforms whatever the topic. This shows the examiner an overall awareness of the topic, rather than just producing well-rehearsed information.

Mark awarded:
AO1 – 9
AO2 – 13
AO3 – 3
Total = 25 out of 25 (100% Grade A)

Seren's essay clearly demonstrates a 'sound' knowledge and understanding with some outstanding use of legal authority.

6. LA4 Section A Strict Liability

Discuss the extent to which the courts insist that all crimes require both an actus reus and a mens rea *(25 marks)*

Tom's answer: Grade C

① The majority of crimes require an actus reus and mens rea. These are a guilty act and a guilty mind. For example, the actus reus for murder is unlawful killing of a human being and the mens reus for murder is malice aforethought, or for GBH it is 'unlawful wounding recklessly or intentionally'. It is the decision of the court to see if there needs to be an actus reus and a mens rea.

② Actus reus means guilty act and in English law it is not a crime to fail to act unless under a duty to do so. There are result crimes which require a certain result to be guilty such as murder where the victim has to die. Or action crimes where the result doesn't matter as in perjury where lying under oath is enough to be convicted even if the lie has no impact on the case. There are also 'duty to act' situations where a person is under a duty to act and if they don't and someone gets injured then they can be guilty of an offence. This is in the case of Pitwood where a train track gate keeper left the gate open when he went on lunch and someone died. He had a duty in his contract to make sure the gate was closed. Also in the case of Miller, a squatter, who lit a cigarette, fell asleep and then woke up with his mattress on fire! He didn't call the fire brigade but moved to the next room and went back to sleep! He had made the dangerous situation and so was under a duty to get help or try to put it out. But only those under a duty to act will have to act.

③ There are also different types of mens rea such as intentionally, recklessly (Cunningham recklessness) or negligence. The type depends on the offence. For murder it has to be intention but you can be reckless to commit a battery.

④ The judge will interpret the statute using statutory interpretation because statutes don't always state whether mens rea is needed. It would be helpful if they did! He must use four tests from the Gammon case to establish if mens rea is needed and start with the test given in B v DPP where they presume mens rea is always needed. Crimes that don't require mens rea are known as strict liability.

⑤ First they ask if the crime is a true crime, as in the case of the landlady who rented her property to people using drugs. She didn't know about this but was still convicted, then on appeal her conviction was quashed. Secondly, they look to see the size of the penalty. Usually small penalties mean strict liability. Thirdly they look to see if the crime is a social concern as in the case Harrow where lottery tickets were sold to underage children. It doesn't matter if they looked over 16. Fourthly they see if the wording of the Act tells them that it is a strict liability offence. Some words like 'cause' in the case of Alphacell v Woodward indicate to the judge that the crime can be strict liability.

⑥ So it can be seen that mens rea and actus reus are very important concepts but the judge has a big role to play. The problem with this is that judges are not elected and might make the wrong decision or there can be some people convicted of the offence and some not. There are different actus reus and mens rea for different offences but with strict liability, offences are designed to regulate behaviour; for example, speeding regulates the flow of traffic. It makes companies more vigilant, which protects lives and the general public. The courts cannot insist that all crimes require an actus reus and mens rea otherwise there would be no deterrent to companies and no safeguard to the public in regards to regulatory behaviour but this is sometimes at the expense of fairness.

Examiner commentary

① Tom has defined the terms actus reus and mens rea as an introduction and given examples of an actus reus and a mens rea.

② Tom has interpreted the question as requiring a discussion of the elements of crime (actus reus and mens rea). Several students took the question to mean this and the mark scheme was amended accordingly to allow the full range of marks for a sound discussion. Here, Tom has focused on omissions and the concept of a 'duty to act'. He generally does this well and shows his understanding through some relevant case law.

③ Again as Tom has misinterpreted the question, he has now moved on to outline the different types of mens rea, which he does at a basic level but with correct use of key terminology.

④ Tom has moved on to correctly consider strict liability, which should have been the focus of his answer. He touches upon the role of the judge in interpreting statutes, which is important. He also squeezes in a lot of important information such as the presumption of mens rea and the four Gammon case tests. These points would have benefited from further explanation but it is good that he has identified these key points in relation to strict liability.

⑤ Tom has discussed, albeit briefly, the four Gammon factors. He has correctly identified them and attempted to use case law to illustrate. He does this briefly and doesn't adequately consider the cases or their implications. This should have been the main focus of his answer along with evaluation of the four factors and how the courts use this guidance to determine if a crime requires both an actus reus and mens rea.

⑥ A nice conclusion by Tom where he has focused well on the question perhaps realising that the question was about strict liability. Ideally no new information should be introduced in a conclusion; it should be a summary of the main body; however, Tom has used it as an opportunity to give some further information about strict liability and the role of judges. He hints at the inconsistency that this approach can give but this could have been further developed if he had the time, along with some cases such as Lim Chin Aik and Smedleys v Breed.

Mark awarded:
AO1 – 7
AO2 – 7
AO3 – 3
Total = 17 out of 25 (68% Grade C)

This is an 'adequate' answer. Despite the question requiring a discussion of strict liability, Tom has taken a slightly different approach, which was not uncommon with students answering this question in the exam. The full range of marks was available to account for this ambiguity but Tom has still produced an 'adequate' answer. He

has taken too broad an approach and not demonstrated a thorough understanding of any one area. This was unfortunately to his detriment with this question. He does demonstrate an understanding of actus reus and duty to act and mentions the types of mens rea but doesn't do this sophisticatedly. He fortunately does move on to strict liability and despite showing an understanding of the presumption of mens read, four factors and some case law, does not develop his points and show depth of understanding. His conclusion, however, is well focused on the question and a nice end.

Seren's answer: Grade A

① It is presumed that all crimes must have an actus reus (guilty act) and a mens rea (guilty mind). However, it is possible for some crimes to have an actus reus only. These are called strict liability crimes. Within this group of crimes are a selection called absolute liability where not only need there not be a mens rea but the actus reus need not even be voluntary.

② In Larsonneur 1933, a French National was deported from England to Ireland. However the Irish authorities would not allow her to stay and she was immediately sent back to England where she was arrested. She was found guilty as she was in England. How she got there (voluntarily or not) was irrelevant. Similarly, in the case of Winzar v Chief Constable of Kent, Winzar was taken to hospital where he was diagnosed as being drunk. He was told to leave the hospital but fell asleep in a corridor. The police were called and walked him to the highway where they arrested him for being 'drunk on the highway'. In the case of Pharmaceutical Company of Great Britain v Storkwain, the pharmacist dispensed drugs from a forged prescription. They did not know it was forged but were still convicted. Their appeal failed.

③ All the above cases illustrate absolute liability which show that the mens rea need not be present and the actus reus need not be voluntary. Looking now at strict liability cases where mens rea is not required. In the case of Gammon (Hong Kong) v Attorney General it was held that the starting point for courts is to presume that mens rea is always needed but that this presumption can be rebutted by considering four factors. In this case, builders had deviated from plans and part of a building fell down. They hadn't meant to deviate or for the building to collapse but that was irrelevant, they had done it and so had the actus reus. The problem with English statutes is that they don't always state that a crime is strict liability or not. It is up to the judge using the questions below and statutory interpretation such as the literal rule or mischief rule to decide. It is important to look at the wording and the intended meaning of Parliament.

④ The four Gammon questions to ask are:

1. Does the statute through the words used imply that it is strict liability? This means, do the words 'intentionally' or 'knowingly' appear in the statute or is it 'cause' or 'possession' which would mean the crime is strict liability. The case of Alphacell v Woodward demonstrate this where a company caused polluted matter to enter into a river. They hadn't meant to do this and had installed a filter which became clogged with leaves but they were the ones who had *caused* it.

2. Is the offence regulatory or a true crime? With regulatory offences there is generally not much stigma attached (e.g. speeding). The case of Sweet v Parsley held that true crimes are criminal and have a stigma attached (such as losing job because of the conviction).

3. Is there a public/social concern aspect to the crime? This may be something like selling alcohol or lottery tickets to those under age as in the case of Harrow v Shah.

4. What is the penalty for the crime? In the case of Gammon there was a £250,000 fine or a 5-year prison sentence but this was very exceptional as the fines are usually small. The smaller the fine (like with speeding) the more likely a case is to be classed as strict liability.

⑤ In some aspects, strict liability can seem unfair as in the case of Callow v Tillstone. The butcher sold bad meat but had asked his vet to check the meat to see if it was fit for human consumption. The vet said it was, so he sold it. However, it was found it was not fit for human consumption and the butcher was fined. The fine was only small but the effect on his reputation must have been a lot greater. He had taken due care but had still committed the actus reus and so was guilty. Nowadays there can be a defence of due diligence for certain offences. Mistake, however, is no defence. A case involving a mistake whilst selling alcohol is Cundy v Le Coq, where it was evident that the person was drunk and shouldn't have been sold alcohol.

⑥ There are various advantages and disadvantages to strict liability. An advantage is that it promotes care and attention but conversely some are convicted even when they have taken all reasonable steps to avoid committing an offence. Larger companies sometimes continue to pay small fines as they have little impact, whereas small companies can be affected both by the fine and damage to their reputation. Once someone realises that there is no defence and courts start imposing larger fines, behaviour will change. A good example of this is wearing seatbelts in cars. Some years ago, lots of people would just not wear a seatbelt but since the law changed and there are lots of fines, most now wear one.

⑦ To look back at the question, it is important to have a consistent approach when it comes to judges determining if a crime requires mens rea or not. Absolute liability crimes seem the most unfair but with strict liability, because it is up to judges, they can also be inconsistent and unfair.

Examiner commentary

① A nice opening paragraph where Seren does well to focus on strict liability and the presumption of mens rea. She also brings in the additional concept of absolute liability offences.

② Seren has correctly identified and considered a range of case law here to illustrate absolute liability. She has done well to get the case titles, facts and conclusion correct. She writes concisely and to the point.

③ I was pleased to see this paragraph included as paragraph 2 (above) on its own, did not explain how the cases demonstrated absolute liability. In this successful paragraph, Seren has correctly explained how the actus reus doesn't need to be voluntary for absolute liability offences. She has then correctly progressed to consider strict liability which is the main focus of this question. She introduces the presumption of mens rea and also the role that judges play using the Gammon guidelines. Her explanation and use of key terminology is very good and she satisfies some of the synoptic requirement by mentioning statutory interpretation and citing some of the rules available.

④ This part of her work is very good indeed with a sophisticated evaluation of the four factors. She includes correct case law and explains their relevance to the concept of strict liability. She gives a good level of depth to show her understanding such as considering a range of words in factor 1 that indicate whether a crime is one of strict liability or not. This gives good focus on the question posed.

⑤ In this paragraph, Seren has considered the fairness of strict liability to enhance her evaluation. She has used a couple of good cases to substantiate her assertions. She brings in mistake as a defence and concludes correctly that it is no defence as there is no mens rea to negate.

⑥ Seren has considered some advantages and disadvantage of strict liability which, though not strictly required for the question, still enhance her answer. She has done well to limit the time she spends on this aspect, which is correct, though she could have brought in the lack of consistency here along with some case law.

⑦ Seren has given a conclusion which is an essential element of an essay question. She has summarised some of the main aspects of

the main body, though it could have been a little longer. She also hints at inconsistency but could have discussed some case law in relation to this earlier in her answer as I have suggested above (e.g. Lim Chin Aik and Smedleys v Breed).

Mark awarded:
AO1 – 9
AO2 – 11
AO3 – 3
Total = 23 out of 25 (92% Grade A)

This is clearly a sound answer where Seren has successfully focused on strict liability and shown a sound knowledge and understanding of the factors that courts consider when determining if a crime is one of strict liability or not. Her answer is enhanced by including absolute liability. She has also included a good range of case law, which she hasn't merely mentioned but considered the implication of in light of the question posed. There were a couple of extra parts to include about lack of consistency and some contrasting case law that might have enabled her to achieve full marks. However, this remains an impressive answer.

7. LA4 Section A Bail

Evaluate the extent to which the law relating to bail maintains a fair balance between the rights of unconvicted defendants and the rights of the general public to be protected against crime. *(25 marks)*

Tom's answer: Grade C

① The law relating to bail is governed by the Bail Act 1976 and the Human Rights Act 1998. The European Convention on Human Rights art 5 guarantees the right to liberty and art 6 the right to a fair trial. The Human Rights Act 1998 incorporated the ECHR into the law of the UK so that when interpreting UK law it should be interpreted with a view to being compatible with human rights.

② There are two types of bail – police bail and court bail. Police bail can be given by the police before or after charge. There are very specific criteria to follow. The custody officer will decide whether to charge or if there is not enough evidence to charge, he can release the suspect on police bail. This could be conditional or unconditional. There is also court bail where the Magistrates decide on whether or not a suspect should be released on bail. There are exceptions where bail should not be granted. These exceptions are when the charge is murder and a person has a previous conviction for a serious case. These defendants used to be automatically denied bail but the case of Caballero challenged this and allowed bail for these defendants in exceptional circumstances.

③ Where there is insufficient evidence to charge, the custody officer would also be allowed to refuse bail if it was necessary to ascertain the name or address of the suspect. They can also refuse it if the suspect might abscond or obstruct the course of justice or if it was necessary for his own protection. If a suspect is given bail certain conditions may be attached. These include the payment of a surety or security, tag, curfew or handing in of a passport. They must also promise to return to the police station or court at a later date.

④ If a person is denied bail, they and their family can suffer in a number of ways such as maybe losing a job, not being able to pay bills and children maybe being taken into care. But it is important that society is taken care of and safe and the best way to do this is to remand a person in custody. It is a balancing act to balance the rights of the defendant with the rights of society to be protected against crime. It breaks a defendant's human rights but it protects the rights of the general public.

Examiner commentary

① Tom introduces his answer very well and references art 5 ECHR the right to liberty to begin to focus on the question posed. This is a good start and he shows a good understanding of the relationship between the EHCR and the HRA 1998.

② Tom does well to outline that there are two types of bail – police and court, though he crucially needed to refer to the presumption in favour of bail under s.4 Bail Act 1976 and police bail under s.38 PACE 1984. These two Acts/sections were key. He also does well to highlight that bail can be conditional or unconditional, which requires further discussion later. He mentions the important case of Caballero briefly but in the correct context. This could have been a more detailed summary of the background to this case and the changes made as a result (with the Crime and Disorder Act 1998).

③ Good summary of some reasons why bail can be refused. There were some more that he needed to include such as the denial of

bail to those addicted to class A drugs who refuse treatment (following the Criminal Justice Act 2003). Good discussion of some conditions that can be attached but again terms such as 'surety' and 'security' could have been explained and Tom could have cited some key cases such as Weddel and Hagans to evaluate the effectiveness of conditions. He could also have focused these examples on the question posed and considered the way that the general public was not protected by the decision to grant these two suspects bail.

④ Tom now realises that he needs to focus on the question posed and this final paragraph is focused on the balance between the rights of suspects and the right of society to be protected. He makes some good points here but this evaluation and focus would have perhaps been better as he went through the essay rather than in his final paragraph as an 'afterthought'. No new information should be included in a conclusion but, rather, it should be a summary of the main body focused on the question.

Mark awarded:
AO1 – 6
AO2 – 7
AO3 – 3
Total = 16 out of 25 (64% Grade C)

This is a lower adequate answer. Tom has shown a good general appreciation of the law on bail and included many key areas but his answer lacks specificity and depth at times. His answer started well by including reference to the Human Rights Act 1998 and art 5 ECHR and the relationship between the two, but he didn't include either of the two main bail statutes (PACE and the Bail Act). These were essential. He generally discusses the reasons for the refusal of bail and includes correct reference to the case of Caballero but needed greater focus on the question. He attempts this focus in the final paragraph but it is a little too late and lacks depth and evaluation.

Seren's answer: Grade A

① Bail at its core is a promise to return and it is deemed necessary for the protection of individual human rights such as the right to liberty under article 5 of the European Convention on Human Rights. This convention has been incorporated into the law of the UK by way of the Human Rights Act 1998 and as a result, our judges are obliged to ensure that convention rights are protected even if that means declaring a UK law as incompatible with human rights. This is something that will be explored in this essay. It will also consider the balance between protecting a suspect's right and protecting the wider society.

② There are two types of bail – police bail and court bail. Police bail falls under s.38 of the Police and Criminal Evidence Act 1984 (PACE) and consists of police bail before charge and police bail after charge. Police bail before charge consists of the accused promising to return at a later date to the police station for questioning, etc. This allows the police the time to investigate further and also gather evidence. A person may be bailed anywhere besides a police station, sometimes known as 'street bail'. This is convenient for the police as it prevents them having to arrest and return to the police station with the suspect and book them in. They can continue with their duties. But there are risks with street bail in that it can be difficult to determine the correct identity. In that respect, it can be seen as not necessarily always protecting the rights of society. Police bail with charge consists of the custody officer determining whether the accused should be bailed after charge depending on how much of a 'risk' they are considered to be. He has the power to impose certain bail conditions such as the accused must reside at a particular address or bail hostel, the accused must refrain from entering a particular area, etc. However, even though a person is thought to be allowed their liberty due to being innocent until proven guilty, a person may be denied bail if they are felt to be a flight risk or a danger to themselves or society.

③ There is also court bail. Under s.4 Bail Act 1976 there is a presumption that everyone should be bailed. This presumption can be rebutted if the accused is likely to abscond or commit an offence whilst on bail. In addition, under the Criminal Justice Act 2003, a person may be denied bail if they have an addiction to a class A drug and refuse treatment. This is due to the fact that the addiction may cause them to steal to pay for their drugs. They will also be refused bail if they are likely to be a risk to themselves or others and the court can take into account any previous convictions. There was a law that said that a person with a

previous serious conviction would be automatically denied bail if he/she was charged with another serious offence. However, the case of Caballero v UK challenged this under art 6 ECHR, which is the right to a fair trial. He felt he would be denied one if he was denied bail automatically. As a result of this case the UK law had to be changed and now those with previous serious convictions can get bail but only in 'exceptional circumstances'.

④ Bail is generally viewed in a positive light as it supports article 5 the right to liberty and the fact that people should be presumed innocent until proven guilty. It allows people to have limited disruption to their personal life whilst allowing the police extra time to do their work or allowing the courts to not fill up prison remand wings. It also ensures the right to a fair trial under art 6 ECHR. However, a downside is that sometimes suspects commit crimes while on bail.

⑤ The courts can impose lots of conditions on bail to try to protect the public and restrict the movement of the suspect. They can require the suspect to pay a security which is a sum of money they pay into court which will be kept by the court on breach of bail conditions or if the defendant absconds. They also accept sureties where a third party guarantees a sum of money that they have to pay if the defendant absconds. But this has not always proved to prevent a suspect committing an offence. This was evident in the case of Weddell an ex-police officer who was accused of killing his wife. He was given bail as his barrister brother acted as a £200,000 surety but on bail, Weddell killed his mother in law and them himself! There are other conditions that can be imposed such as an injunction telling the suspect not to go to a particular area, surrender of passport and a curfew or tag. The case of R v Hagans again shows how ineffective these conditions can be in protecting the public. He had 28 previous convictions for violent and sexual offences yet was given bail. He was told not to go to Cheltenham but on bail he raped and killed a woman in Gloucester. The conditions were ineffective and he should have been remanded.

⑥ In conclusion, bail is a right and it protects the human rights of liberty and a fair trial. The courts try to impose conditions that would prevent a person being able to commit crime but they don't always work as seen above with the cases of Hagans and Weddel. However, if a person is remanded and doesn't get bail, they can suffer greatly as can their family who have done nothing wrong themselves. It is a fine balancing act and the courts don't always get it right.

Examiner commentary

① An excellent introduction is provided by Seren. She has put her answer in context by correctly explaining the relationship between bail and the ECHR and between the ECHR and HRA 1998. She also does well to signpost to the reader what the essay is going to consider, which is an excellent way to approach an introduction. She also ensures her introduction focuses on the question posed and the conflict between the rights of a suspect and the rights of the general public.

② Both court bail and police bail were required for this question and Seren has identified both in this paragraph. In addition, she clearly explains police bail, citing the appropriate statute and section. She shows a wider understanding by explaining the purpose of police bail, the factors taken into account in determining if a suspect should get police bail and evaluates the effectiveness of street bail in light of the question posed.

③ Similar to the paragraph above and logically working through the issues, Seren has here progressed on to court bail. She includes the important presumption of the right to bail and the factors the court takes into account. She enhances her answer by further citation of the CJA 2003 and the issue of bail for drug addicts. Excellent and relevant use of the Caballero case which Seren has explained well and showed sound knowledge and understanding.

④ Good focus in this paragraph on the question posed bringing in the human rights aspect. Seren gives a balanced discussion from both the public's view and the suspect's.

⑤ An excellent paragraph outlining and explaining some of the main conditions on bail and how they attempt to prevent a person from offending whilst on bail. Good use of two key cases as authority on the issue of conditions being somewhat ineffective.

⑥ A concise and appropriate conclusion here where Seren has summarised some of the main body of her work. She uses it as an

opportunity to focus on the question posed and cites earlier mentioned legal authority to give weight to her conclusion – an effective ending.

Mark awarded:
AO1 – 9
AO2 – 13
AO3 – 3
Total = 25 out of 25 (100% Grade A)

This is clearly a 'sound' answer. Seren has taken a logical path through the essay with a clear structure. The answer started very well and she focused on the question well throughout. These 25-mark essays can be difficult to structure and focus but she deals very well with the amount of information she needs to include and she is selective on what she spends her time on, which is important when there is a limited word count. An excellent range of legal authority is included, which is not merely mentioned but explained fully and evaluated in light of the question. This is a very good answer, especially considering the time constraint and exam conditions.

8. LA4 Section B Sentencing

a) Explain the purpose of non-court alternatives as punishments for young offenders *(11 marks)*

Tom's answer: Grade C

① Under the Children and Young Persons Act 1933, a Youth Court was put in place to separate those offenders aged 10-17 from adults.

② Aside from the Youth Court, which replaces the Magistrates' Court in cases involving a defendant aged between 10 and 17, there are also non-court alternatives as punishments for young offenders. The purpose of these non-court alternatives is to prevent further crime but in a way that is seen as more appropriate for children.

③ Final Warnings are given to young offenders to stop them from re-offending without going through the distress of court. They act as a deterrent because if the child re-offends the next step will be court. It is a deterrent to stop the children from partaking in further offences.

④ Another non-court alternative given to youths is the anti-social behaviour order, given for minor offences such as graffiti and to youths who are acting anti-socially, which could include disturbances. Although an ASBO is not a Final Warning, it can deter the youth from offending again.

⑤ Young offenders aged 16 or 17 can be given penalty notices for disorder – the purpose of these is retribution as it is a way of punishing the youth for the offence. It can be added that the purpose of non-court alternatives is to save time and money.

⑥ Overall, the non-court alternatives can be beneficial and they can work; however, it can be added that sometimes the purpose of them is not fulfilled because they are not seen as serious enough punishment. Non-court settlements favour rehabilitation and try to change the behaviour of the youth instead of incapacitation.

Examiner commentary

① ② A basic insight into purposes of sentencing for young offenders. There is a lack of legal terminology; for example, words such as deterrence, rehabilitation. Candidates should try, wherever possible, to use legal terms in their correct context to provide an articulate response.

③ Final Warnings are explained in terms of their aim; this time with greater use of legal terminology. However, missing is an explanation of what a Final Warning is and the circumstances under which one can be given. This would be necessary to take the AO1 of Knowledge and Understanding element above 'limited'.

④ A relatively good explanation of ASBOs, but there is a distinct lack of substance as to the merits of an ASBO – for example, the fact that they are seen by some youths as a 'trophy' and are not very successful in achieving their aim.

⑤ Penalty Notices for Disorder are discussed here in limited detail, with the focus on their purpose, not what they are. Even though the question is asking about the purpose of these disposals, the explanation of what they are and for what they can be given is crucial to then explaining the purpose of them. Tom has neglected to talk about Reprimands as a non-court alternative and since the source makes reference to these, they are expected in the answer.

Marks awarded:
AO1 – 5
AO3 – 1
Total= 6 out of 11 (55% Grade D)

This is a limited answer at best, and is lacking the legal substance to venture into a higher band of marks. There is little or no evaluative content and the knowledge of the various out of court disposals is unconvincing.

Seren's answer: Grade A

① There are five main purposes of sentencing under the Criminal Justice Act 2003. These are: deterrence, reform, protection of the public, reparation and punishment. Where young offenders are concerned, they are most concerned with reform, knowing what they have done wrong so they won't do it again. Also, another objective is to deter young offenders from re-offending.

② The most common form of sentence for a young offender are the non-court options which offer non-custodial sentences. These are the likes of reprimands, final warnings, anti-social behavior orders. These are given to young offenders for low level crimes such as graffiti, petty theft and are given to the offenders by the local council and the local police.

③ The non-court alternatives are mainly concerned with reprimanding the young offenders by giving them a second chance. The likes of ASBOs mean they can't go to certain places or go out at certain times. These help the children to reflect on what they have done wrong. Also with the final warnings the next step is to go to the Youth Court and can result in them receiving a custodial sentence. For some youths this will have a positive effect, but for some it will not.

④ The main advantages of these are so they can have a second chance and not get sent to court, which for a child can be intimidating. These orders are warning signs to both children and their parents and will prompt the parents to address their child's behaviour before they start committing more serious crimes. These orders do not result in the youth having a criminal record, so that it will not affect their future chances of education and employment. ASBOs and Reprimands will be placed on a young offender for between one and two years.

⑤ Despite the advantages, there are negative aspects, too. Some youths see the ASBO as a good thing, an order of which they are proud. Also, as they are not given a custodial sentence or been to court they do not know what they have done, so may not be deterred. Some youths will need the experience of going to court or a young offenders' institution in order to reform their behaviour. Also, a lot of youths follow in their parents' footsteps, if they have grown up in a criminal family. This means the purposes of these non-court alternatives are not always achieved.

Examiner commentary

① An excellent introduction showing an understanding of the general principles of sentencing with current and relevant legal authority. This immediately tells the examiner that there is an understanding of the question and what it requires. Inclusion of the Criminal Justice Act 2003 would make this introduction almost flawless. The introduction is the first hint to the examiner of the level of understanding, so it is important that it is as memorable as possible.

② In this paragraph, Seren puts the whole answer into context, referring to the question and outlining the types of crime that can be dealt with by an out of court disposal. What could improve this is by citing the relevant legal authority, under which each disposal falls – for example, the Referral Order is found under ss.16–28 Powers of Criminal Courts (Sentencing) Act 2000.

③ Seren gives a good outline here of ASBOs and Final Warnings. Sometimes it is necessary to state the obvious; in this case giving a basic explanation of the use of these sentences shows the examiner the depth of knowledge and a good basis from which evaluation can then progress. Disappointingly, not all the disposals referred to in the source are explained – Seren could have expanded further on this with more detail. Crucially though, she has begun to evaluate the disposals, which helps answer the question in terms of whether the 'purpose' of the disposals has been achieved.

④ This paragraph continues evaluating out of court disposals, with further indication of an in-depth knowledge and convincing the examiner of a 'sound' knowledge.

⑤ This paragraph makes the answer balanced because here Seren has discussed the more negative aspects of out of court disposals and shows an insight into social aspects of justice.

Mark awarded:
AO1 – 7
AO3 – 2
Total = 9 out of 11 (82% Grade A)

A good insight here, with a definite 'sound' knowledge, although it is a little askew in terms of structure. An idea for a structure for this type of question could be:

1 Introduction – Aims of sentencing for youths, with reference to the Criminal Justice Act 2003.

2 An explanation of EVERY out of court disposal mentioned in the source, and how they are used (if there is no source, draw on your own knowledge).

3 Positive aspects of these disposals – do they achieve their purpose?

4 Negative aspects of these disposals – how do they not achieve their purpose?

b) Evaluate the role of the Crown Court when dealing with young offenders. *(14 marks)*

Tom's answer: Grade C

① Typically, young offenders are tried in the Youth Court, which is a court that sits off the Magistrates' Court. However, the Crown Court also has a role in trying young offenders.

② In cases involving severe crime, for example murder or rape, even if the defendant is a youth, he will be tried in the Crown Court. For instance in the case of Venables and Thompson, although the boys were under 16, the case was tried in the Crown Court because of its severity. The boys were charged with the murder of toddler Jamie Bulger. It is argued that even in severe cases involving children, the case should stay in the Youth Court, but the opposite can also be argued.

③ The Crown Court also deals with appeals from the Youth Court; it deals with appeals on conviction and sentencing. This is good because the Crown Court deals with criminal law and therefore has the knowledge to deal with these appeals. On the other hand, it could be argued that they do not have sufficient knowledge to deal with those offenders who are under 18.

Examiner commentary

① A vague introduction – here, Tom needs to be more convincing and outline when the Crown Court is used for youths – that is, when the case is too serious for the Youth Court or when the youth is being tried alongside an adult. It may also be useful to define what a 'youth' is for the purposes of the law. It would also be refreshing to see an explanation as to the reasons why a young offender may be sent to the Crown Court; primarily because the Youth Court is run by specially trained Magistrates who do not have the legal knowledge required for certain cases.

② Excellent citation here of the Thompson and Venables case – this is a key case in the use of the Youth Court for indictable offences committed by youths. It may be useful here to also mention Article 6 ECHR – right to a fair trial. Candidates should be constantly reminded that Human Rights is an underpinning principle of the whole specification so should be mentioned at any given opportunity. It may also be recommended here to talk about the powers the Youth Court has in terms of sentencing an offender.

③ There is a broad knowledge here of appeals, which is indeed a function of the Crown Court, but there is very limited evaluation.

Tom has shown no evidence of evaluation, which would be expected to achieve anywhere near the full complement of 14 marks.

Mark awarded:
AO2 – 6
AO3 – 1
Total = 7 out of 14 (50% Grade D)

Tom's answer demonstrates no more than 'limited' knowledge, because the question was not answered thoroughly and the 'evaluate' element was not attempted. The importance of command words should not be overlooked – read the question and make sure all elements are covered in the answer.

Seren's answer: Grade A

① When a young offender is made to go to court, the vast majority will have to go to the Youth Court, which is part of the Magistrates' Court. Here they mainly give Referral Orders, Reparation Orders or Youth Rehabilitation Orders, which are all non-custodial. The only custodial sentence a Youth Court can give is a Detention and Training Order of between 2 and 24 months. Despite this, a minority of young offenders are sent to the Crown Court for more serious offences.

② A young person will be tried in the Crown Court if the charge is murder, death by dangerous driving, or if there is a co-defendant who is an adult. At the Crown Court, they will be given a custodial sentence. The types of custodial sentence children receive from the Crown Court are section 90 orders where a child is convicted of murder, as they will be detained indefinitely 'At Her Majesty's Pleasure'. Also a section 91 Order is available and these are given to youths who have committed a crime which carries a sentence of up to 14 years in custody. They can also give out Detention and Training Orders under the Powers of Criminal Courts (Sentencing) Act 2000 for between 2 and 24 months. Here they will spend half their time in detention and the other half in training or education. They learn the National Curriculum for 25 hours a week, so it helps them with their rehabilitation on release. When a child is given a custodial sentence they will most likely spend their time in a young offenders institute or local authority accommodation.

③ When a child is tried in the Crown Court, it is very different to how an adult would be tried. The judge and barristers do not wear wigs and gowns, no complex language is used, the children will stand near their parents or carers and they will not be elevated. Also before the trial they will have had the opportunity to look around the court and be told how proceedings will commence. This is because of the case of Thompson and Venables who were tried and convicted of the murder of Jamie Bulger. In court, they were elevated so the whole court could see them, the judges and barristers spoke in a way they could not understand and there were wigs and gowns. Also, their parents were seated across the other side of the court room. This initiated changes so youths are not intimidated and therefore less chance of them admitting a crime because they are daunted. This will also prevent a breach of Article 6 ECHR.

④ The Crown Court's role when dealing with young offender is similar to the way in which they deal with adults; to find the truth using a judge and jury and sentence them appropriately. Despite this, the way in which the proceedings are conducted is different for youths and will be more appropriate to achieve a fair trial.

Examiner commentary

① A good introduction showing the powers of the Youth Court. All relevant disposals are mentioned to signpost the rest of the answer and allow for expansion. This shows a good structure and an in-depth knowledge.

② This is an excellent paragraph; again Seren convincing the examiner that she has an in-depth knowledge of the topic. The sentences given by the court to youths are explained in detail, crucially with legal authority. A detailed knowledge and understanding is apparent in the explanations given of the sentences available and of the functions of the Crown Court in terms of youths. All the major sentences are discussed – s.90/s.91/ Detention and Training Orders.

③ This is a crucial paragraph in answering the question, because Seren shows knowledge of how the court operates, which then allows for evaluation. The vital case of Thompson and Venebles is mentioned, with reference to art 6 ECHR. This provides suitable evaluation, because Seren is showing that the Crown Court does operate within the realms of the right to a fair trial. Other points of evaluation that could have been included are: positively, that serious offences should be tried with a jury in a Crown Court regardless of the age of the defendant. This concept has its roots in the Magna Carta. Further, a negative aspect that could be discussed is that even though much has been done to improve the experience for youths in Crown Court, it is still a very traumatic experience and begs the question, should youths ever be subjected to a criminal trial? The provisions for youths at the Crown Court that Seren mentions are key to answering the question; the legal authority for these provisions comes from a Practice Direction issued in 2000 by the then Lord Chief Justice, Lord Bingham.

④ A rounded conclusion, again making reference to the human rights aspects of the Crown Court in trying youths.

Mark awarded:
AO2 – 13
AO3 – 1
Total = 14 out of 14 (100% Grade A)

This is a confident answer, showing a definite 'sound' knowledge of the workings of the Crown Court in relation to youths. Crucially, Seren has stuck to the question and channelled her response into youths; it is a very common mistake for candidates to have approached this question as a general Crown Court question, and completely missed the point about youth offenders.

Index